POWER OUTAGE

But you will receive power when the Holy Spirit has come upon you, and you will be my witnesses in Jerusalem and in all Judea and Samaria, and to the end of the earth.
Acts 1:8 (ESV)

POWER OUTAGE

BY

Rob Gross

Paul L. Cox

POWER OUTAGE
By Rob Gross & Paul L. Cox

Aslan's Place Publications
9315 Sagebrush Street
Apple Valley, CA 92308
760-810-0990
aslansplace.com

Scriptures are taken from:

The ESV® Bible (The Holy Bible, English Standard Version®) copyright © 2001 by Crossway Bible, a publishing ministry of Good News Publishers. Used by permission. All rights reserved.

The New King James Version (NKJV): New King James Version®. Copyright © 1982 by Thomas Nelson, Inc., publishers. Used by permission. All rights reserved.

The Holy Bible, New International Version® NIV® Copyright © 1973, 1978, 1984, 2011 by Biblica, Inc.™ Used by permission. All rights reserved worldwide.

Scripture quotations marked TPT are from The Passion Translation®. Copyright © 2017 by BroadStreet Publishing® Group, LLC. Used by permission. All rights reserved. thePassionTranslation.com.

ISBN: 979-8-3328-9353-7
Printed in the United States of America

TABLE OF CONTENTS

PROPHETIC WORD

Note: When this word was received, Larry said, "It felt like I connected to the Angel over the Kingdom Institute, which surprised me some:"

It's time to come and behold the appearing of the supremacy of The Son.

This is the hour of the unveiling of The Eternal Power. Yes, the power at My right hand is beginning to stand up within My Body, My governmental branch united with the Living Tree that is The Greater One.

I will awaken your true authentic, redeemed life and you will be a pillar of power that will shower the Earth with the light of The Father's face. Come and run the race with Me and I will anoint your eyes to see that there is an upgrade of My brilliance coming to the earth. It will be so unprecedented that it will quake the earth awake at the unveiling of the stature and the supremacy of The Spirit of Sonship. This will shake structures and remove ancient evil schemes.

So let your heart be turned toward the revealing and the healing by the power that is with Me at My right hand. Come and Behold Me.

Larry Pearson
https://www.lionswordsolutions.ca

FOREWORD

My dear friends, Rob Gross and Paul L Cox, have done it again! In addition to previously establishing The Kingdom Institute and co-authoring several books in the *Exploring Heavenly Places* series as well as *The Revelation of the Vault: Provision for the Vision*, they've now produced another life-changing book, *Power Outage*.

Speaking to His disciples, Jesus made a comment that blows my mind:

> *Truly, truly, I say to you, whoever believes in me will also do the works that I do; and greater works than these will he do, because I am going to the Father.*[1]

Perhaps, the initial outpouring of the Holy Spirit at Pentecost was a taste or first fruit of that promise; but since none of us were eyewitness to that, it's kind of hard to know for sure. To date, this has not happened in our lifetime. Why? We believe it is in large part because the Church – the Body of Christ – is suffering from a power-of-God outage. Why again? Perhaps it's because as much as we speak and teach about His power, we really don't have an experiential, or *yada*, knowing of it. But good news! *Power Outage* goes into detail about how to flip the switch back on in order to get His power flowing in our lives as never before. Then, when God's timing is right, perhaps we will be privileged to see the fulfillment of Jesus' prophetic promise.

Rob, senior pastor of Mountain View Community Church in Kaneohe, Hawaii, and Paul, co-founder of Aslan's Place in Apple Valley California, live what they write. As a result, this book is very much a personal account of how:

1) They've witnessed God's miracle-working power firsthand
2) They have experienced His power through discernment
3) The power has changed their lives, and those of others

As always, what you see/read is what you get with both Rob and Paul. With great humility, they credit God for His marvelous works and make it abundantly clear that He is their strength, and their source of inspiration and blessing. For those who are fortunate enough to know Rob and Paul personally, or who've either read their books or heard them teach, *Power Outage* will be a real treat because some of their favorite experiences and/or stories are written down for all to enjoy.

Barbara Kain Parker
Standing in Faith Ministries
https://standinginfaithministries.com

---

[1] John 14:12

INTRODUCTION

ROB GROSS

Jesus made an astounding statement in John 14:12 that His disciples (meaning all who would follow Him down through the centuries) would do greater works than He performed during His three-year ministry. Wow! To say that we would perform greater miracles than He did is mind blowing! I don't know what your personal response to that statement is, but I have chosen to literally believe it.

To encourage you to believe God for greater things, this introduction has been set aside to share the amazing account of how the Lord performed a bonafide, medically confirmed miracle through everyday people like you and me on behalf of a twelve-year-old boy who had been diagnosed with a rare form of cancer.

As told by his dad, Jeff Kimbrel:

In early November 2022, a doctor took samples of an abscess on my son Dezmond's gum. The doctor told us not to worry about cancer because oral cancer does not occur in eleven-year-old children.

On November 11, 2022, I got the worst news of my life when I received a call from Dezmond's oral surgeon. The doctor asked, "Jeff, are you home? Are you sitting down?" "No, I'm not." "If you want to go home, I can call you back." "Absolutely not; please tell me now." The doctor said. "Dezmond has cancer."

I stuffed down my emotions and asked Dr. Nishimoto questions about Dez's treatment, as if my son was a car. It was all I could do to maintain composure. Dr. Nishimoto explained that he spoke with the doctor he did his residency under in Seattle. They agreed Dezmond would need surgery to remove all of his teeth and gums below the upper left jawbone. Part of his palate would also need to be removed. Additionally, a piece of Dezmond's leg bone would replace his jawbone and palate, and a skin graft would be used to cover it. Dezmond would also need a neck dissection to remove his lymph nodes, which would result in a sizable scar. A prosthesis would replace his caved-in facial features and teeth, but even with these procedures he would have a slight deformity. After these treatments he would begin chemotherapy.

Soon after, we began to worry about Dez's future. Would there be a 'next few years'? Could he go to school? Would these procedures stunt his growth? Would he be able to box? What about his guitar lessons? What impact would this ordeal have on him mentally? My wife and I had so many plans for our son and now everything was spiraling out of control.

Finding God at DVG Jiu Jitsu:
During the early fall 2022, I received an advertisement for a new Brazilian Jiu Jitsu school on my Facebook feed. Professor (black belt instructor) Brandon Gross was making the pitch. I knew him as a K-Team BJJ instructor in Kaneohe. He had a great reputation and taught a Friday family class that had a great logo of a father holding his son on his shoulders. I explored the webpage and saw that there was another instructor,

Professor Garrett Whitman at DVG Jiu Jitsu. I signed up for an appointment to meet both professors and was a new student by the end of the meeting. A couple of weeks later, before the DVG grand opening day event, we received Dezmond's diagnosis. I texted Professor Brandon that I had a family emergency, and it would not be possible for me to attend, congratulated them on the opening, and said I would follow up the following week.

I called Brandon later that week and told him that my boy had cancer. I felt defeated in every way. I continued to tell him I wanted to come to class, but I might be a bit of a mess. Brandon listened. He knew I needed help and asked if we could pray. He asked for God's guidance and strength for my wife and I, for Dezmond's healing, and for courage in the trials ahead. When I arrived at school for class, both Professors Garrett and Brandon received me. They both let me lean on them with my pain. Garrett emphasized the importance of prayer and Brandon said that his church was praying for Dezmond.

So rare, the first of its kind:
On November 30, Dezmond and I arrived in Seattle for a series of consultations with a specialist. After more tests, Dez's surgery was scheduled for December 14th. While waiting, we received more information about Dezmond's tumor. It was a rare form of squamous cell carcinoma called a "carcinoma cuniculatum". There were only ten cases of this particular cancer, but never an oral cancer. All ten had been skin cancers. Nothing about this made sense, and Dezmond's case was shared throughout the American and UK

Pathology community without any returns or insights. To compound this, multiple boards of pathologists were having a difficult time agreeing given the specifics. Signing off on the cancer diagnosis so treatment could go forward would have been a first for any of them. It was perceived as a professional risk.

On December 14th, Dezmond had five teeth, with gum, removed. They cut the tumor out with the teeth/gums but refrained from going further. They sent the samples to UW and UCSF for testing and for review from a several pathology boards. I was relieved that they did not do the entire surgery, but they left a plate in Dezmond's mouth covering the surgery site. Later, the plate was removed, and his doctor confirmed the diagnosis of cancer.

The following weekend was Christmas and we decided to go home. The next week his Seattle doctor called and said that she hurt her shoulder in a slip and the operation would be postponed until January 20th. She said she was cancelling all of her surgeries except Dez's.

A message of hope from a friend:
Moments before we left for the airport on January 17th to return to Seattle for Dez's second surgery, a friend from DVG Jiu Jitsu messaged me saying, "I have faith in God, and know that He's a God of restoration." God spoke directly to our family through this friend delivering a message of hope, respite, and restoration.

Crying out to God:

I confess that I have never been to church voluntarily. I was baptized while attending a Lutheran school and later chaperoned youth for services at the Vineyard in Boise, Idaho.

I listened to Garrett and Brandon and spent a lot of time praying. At least I hope it was praying. It was not eloquent or measured words, but words mostly driven by fear. I cried out, "Please, God, not my boy! Please don't take my son!" I was not very good at praying, but I wanted that connection. I tried to express myself better. I relaxed and might have called Jesus, "Dude", a few times. I asked Him to help me be a better person, swallowed my pride, and apologized for some of my previous attitudes and behaviors.

During this difficult time God helped me explore the idea of forgiving others and letting go of bitterness which had always been a struggle for me. Wanting to go forward down this path and wanting Dez to have hope, I decided we should start going to church before the surgery. On Sunday, February 19th we attended Mountain View Community Church for the first time. Dezmond was called forward to receive prayer from the elders and any who felt led to pray for him. While Dezmond was being anointed with oil by Pastor Rob someone pressed a vial of oil into my hand. Little did I know what the Lord was planning to do.

God was with us:
When we arrived in Seattle for the February 27th surgery, Dez wept. He had been incredibly brave throughout his ordeal, and I could not imagine what he was going through.

At the hospital Dez was prepped and anesthetized for surgery. As he drifted off, we told him we loved him and that he would be all right. As Dez was about to be wheeled into the surgical room I took out the cylinder of oil that had been handed to me a week earlier. I had opened it days earlier and smelled the wood oil flower scent. While praying for Dez I felt led to anoint him. I leaned over and kissed him on the top of his head I noticed that oil was already on his forehead. The Lord had already anointed my son! Following His lead, I dabbed my finger with oil and traced a line on his forehead before the nurses took him.

The Lord watched over my son that day. He showed me that He was actually with my son and in control of his life. I profoundly see this now and want to live my life in such way that shows my deepest appreciation, follows His path for me and draws my family closer to Him.

The miracle:
While we were waiting near the cafeteria, Dez's doctor approached us and said that she had cut a wide area of Dez's gum and sent it to San Francisco State University for testing. Apparently, when she had opened his gum, the cancer was no longer visible. The results came back from SFSU stating that there were no genetic markers for cancer in the samples. My wife and I were overjoyed but confused. The doctor said that she was still having some genetic disorders ruled out, but the gum was free of cancer. She then added that she would run the same tests again to be sure.

We stayed a few more days in Seattle until the second test results returned. They were also negative for cancer and any genetic disorders. She checked Dez's lymph nodes, and they were clear. She then told us that Dez would need a follow up MRI in a few months and regular visits to Seattle (Dez's first follow up visit six months later showed, once again, that there was no cancer in his gum).

Second chance and renewed hope:
We came home to a second chance and renewed hope. Dez still has some bumps ahead, but we are trusting God and grateful that he is a healthy teenage boy. I thank God every day for being with Dez when he was helpless and delivering him back to us.

On March 5th we attended MVCC to testify that Dez is cancer free. Mahalo (thanks) to Pastor Rob, Pastor Brandon, Professor Garrett, the aunty who gave Dez the prophetic watercolor picture (it is hanging in his room), the aunty who handed me the oil, and everyone at MVCC. I appreciate you all and am grateful for a home in which to worship, learn, and serve.

Reflections:
Where is the power in the Church today to heal the sick – the power that was evident in the Gospels, the Book of Acts and in Dezmond Kimbrel's life? And why aren't more churches training and empowering their people to heal the sick and perform extraordinary miracles?

The Bible clearly tells us that supernatural healing is available to believers and pre-believers alike. Yet, this raises the perplexing question, "Why do some faith-filled believers who have received heart-felt, anointed prayer along with top notch medical care continue to be sick and infirm?" To be honest, I don't have a clear-cut cookie cutter explanation for why the Lord doesn't answer some people's cries for healing. I have learned however, that healing the sick is extremely complex in nature and can be hindered, if not altogether blocked, when the enemy has been given the legal right to keep individuals in a sickly state.

Paul Cox and I have written this book to encourage you to believe God for your breakthrough and to explain why we believe the enemy keeps Holy Spirit-filled believers in physical bondage. Although not exhaustive, this book provides a biblical starting point for Christians to break free from the devil's schemes and tap into the Holy Spirit's supernatural power that can effect tangible, medically confirmed healing.

Hebrews 13:5 tells us that Jesus is the same today, yesterday and forever. This means that the First Century Jesus who healed the sick and performed breath-taking miracles is still doing the same today. Many pastors, divine healers and authors have chronicled and confirmed the reality of the healing ministry of Jesus over the centuries. In spite of this, much of the wider church of Christ has not experienced the miracles and wonders of the Holy Spirit. This is changing today as a wave of healing is moving across the globe to draw people like Jeff Kimbrel to Jesus.

Our aim in this book, is to investigate two things: 1) What are some of the common legal rights the enemy has in his arsenal to keep people sick, and 2) Why is the church suffering from a power outage?

CHAPTER ONE:
THE ENEMY IS A LEGALIST
ROB GROSS

A legalist is someone who adheres to a legal code. The devil knows the Word of God (the divine legal code) front and back and jumps at any opportunity we give him to infiltrate our mind, will and emotions when we violate God's blueprint for living. When a believer breaks the commands of God, he gives Satan's horde the 'green' light to demonically influence them in varying degrees (Mark 5:15; 7:25; 9:17; Luke 4:33; 8:27; John 10:20-21; Acts 8:7; 16:16; 19:13).

This of course raises the theological issue that many believers ask, "Can a Christian have a demon?" Many believers ask this question based on 2 Corinthians 5:17:

> *Therefore, if anyone is in Christ, he is a new creation. The old has passed away; behold, the new has come. (ESV)*

Those who refer to this passage along with Galatians 6:12-16, believe that when we receive Jesus as our Lord and Savior we are washed inside and out and therefore completely cannot have a demon. Although I wish this perspective was true, it is not.

Recently I spoke with an anointed deliverance minister who confirmed that a believer can have a demon when he ministered to a Christian along with a group of intercessors. Wanting to illustrate that a believer can be demonized he engaged the spirit he was confronting with the question, "Where are you?" The demon replied under the authority of Christ, "I'm inside of his body." The deliverance minister persisted, "You know what I'm referring to, "Where exactly are you?" The demon spoke, "I'm in his soul." The deliverance minister asked one more question, "Are you in his spirit?" And the demon answered, "I can't be there because the other GUY is there."

Demons when given the legal right, can occupy a Christian's body and soul (mind, will and emotions), but they cannot take up residence in a believer's spirit because this is where the Holy Spirit dwells. When we receive Christ, the Lord immediately inhabits our spirit, but He still takes us through the process of sanctification (setting us apart for holy use as our soul is cleansed from evil and we obey the Word of God and grow in Christlike character).

Years ago, I was asked to pray for a Christian leader who was dealing with liver issues. I asked him, "Have you or someone in your generational line ever committed adultery?" He replied, "Yes"; so, I directed him to Proverbs 7:21-23 (ESV):

> **With much seductive speech she persuades him; with her smooth talk she compels him. All at once he follows her, as an ox goes to the slaughter, or as a stag is caught fast till an arrow pierces its liver; as a bird rushes into a snare; he does not know that it will cost him his life.**

Having violated Exodus 20:14, *"You shall not commit adultery,"* this leader had given the enemy the legal right to attack his liver. To God's glory, the man repented and renounced the sin of adultery for himself and his family line. As far as I know, his liver is in good working order years later.

Delivered to the Torturers:

Over the years I have interacted with believers who have struggled to forgive those who have hurt or offended them. As someone who has dealt with the same struggle, I point them to Matthew 18:21-34:

> *Then Peter came to Him and said, "Lord, how often shall my brother sin against me, and I forgive him? Up to seven times?" Jesus said to him, "I do not say to you, up to seven times, but up to seventy times seven. Therefore the kingdom of heaven is like a certain king who wanted to settle accounts with his servants. And when he had begun to settle accounts, one was brought to him who owed him ten thousand talents. But as he was not able to pay, his master commanded that he be sold, with his wife and children and all that he had, and that payment be made. The servant therefore fell down before him, saying, 'Master, have patience with me, and I will pay you all.' Then the master of that servant was moved with compassion, released him, and forgave him the debt. So his fellow servant fell down at his feet and begged him, saying, 'Have patience with me, and I will pay you all.' "*

> *But that servant went out and found one of his fellow servants who owed him a hundred denarii; and he laid hands on him and took by the throat, saying, 'Pay me what you owe!' And he would not, but went and threw him into prison till he should pay the debt. So when his fellow servants saw what had been done, they were very grieved, and came and told their master all that had been done. Then his master, after he had called him, said to him,*

'You wicked servant! I forgave you all that debt because you begged me. Should you not also have had compassion on your fellow servant, just as I had pity on you?' And his master was angry, and delivered him to the torturers until he should pay all that was due to him. "So My heavenly Father also will do to you if each of you, from his heart, does not forgive his brother his trespasses." (NKJV)

When a believer fails to forgive a brother for an offense he is delivered over to the torturers, jailers or tormentors (the demonic realm). According to the Lord, if we refuse to forgive those who have hurt us, we will not receive His forgiveness (Matthew 6:15) thus blocking His healing power.

So, here's the deal: To ensure the free flow of God's supernatural power, we need to ask the Holy Spirit to reveal the enemy's legal right that is blocking us from being healed (I will share 18 reasons why people don't get healed in Chapter Seven).

In the introduction of this book, I referred to an astounding miracle that the Lord performed for a twelve-year-old boy with a rare gum cancer, who remains healed to this day. I'd like now to briefly share about a woman in our congregation who the Lord healed of stage 4 cancer after being prayed over by the elders of our church, only to see the cancer return 8 months later.

Feeling badly because the cancer returned, she apologized to me because she had shared on resurrection Sunday that God had healed her. I quickly encouraged her not to feel bad, explaining that the cancer had returned because the enemy had the legal right to stir it up again. I then reassured her that we were committed to help her not only discover the enemy's legal right, but to pray for her until the cancer completely left her body.

Experienced fishermen normally have a large tackle box of shiny lures to hook and catch different kinds of fish. Likewise, Satan has a large tackle box of hooks that he uses to bait believers into giving him the legal right to access their thoughts, wills and emotions. Let's explore next how the enemy does this.

How Does Satan Gain Legal Access?
Common entry points to be explained in detail:

1. Sex outside of marriage
2. Sexual victimization
3. Having an abortion
4. Refusing to forgive
5. Going to bed angry
6. Making blood covenants
7. Yoga and dabbling in the occult
8. Making inner vows
9. Adverse childhood experiences
10. Generational sin

(1) Sex Outside of Marriage: I want to make one thing clear. God is not against sex! After all, He invented it. What a great God! The Lord's intent has been for husbands and wives to connect on a very deep, intimate level through sexual intercourse. Sex is a gift from God but is to be enjoyed within the protective confines of marriage. Any time one has sex outside of marriage in an adulterous relationship, with a family member, with an animal, or in homosexual or heterosexual sexual encounter, it gives the devil a legal right to infiltrate their soul (mind, will and emotions) resulting in demonization (harassment) and unhealthy sexual ties.

Our Papa does not want us to succumb to the schemes of darkness because He knows the debilitating ramifications when we do so. This is why He has warned us in His word to stay clear of sexual immorality (1 Thessalonians 4:3). In Leviticus 18:20-28 the Lord exhorted His people out of His great love and concern for them to avoid sexual liaisons that would result in the land 'vomiting' them out:

> *And you shall not lie sexually with your neighbor's wife and so make yourself unclean with her. You shall not give any of your children to offer them to Molech, and so profane the name of your God: I am the Lord. And you shall not lie sexually with your neighbor's wife and so make yourself unclean with her. You shall not lie with a male as with a woman; it is an abomination. And you shall not lie with any animal and so make yourself unclean with it, neither shall any woman give herself to an animal to lie with it: it is perversion. "Do not make yourselves unclean by any of these things, for by all these the nations I am driving out before you have become unclean, and the land became unclean, <u>so that I punished its iniquity, and the land vomited out its inhabitants</u>. But you shall keep my statutes and my rules and do none of these abominations, either the native or the stranger who sojourns among you (for the people of the land, who were before you, did all of these abominations, so that the land became unclean), lest the land vomit you out when you make it unclean, as it vomited out the nation that was before you."(ESV)*

What does 'vomiting out' mean? Regularly hooking up with others outside of marriage in any context will lead to a life filled with struggle including being unable to break free from past partners (soul ties), acquiring STD's and succumbing to the spirit of rejection. But there's a more serious ramification. According to Leviticus 18:20-28 sex outside the marriage bed causes the land where we live to issue us a divorce decree (see above). This spiritual transaction where the land where we live rejects us, affects our ability to put down roots where we live and inhibits us from walking in God's purpose and plan for our lives. When the devil has legal access to our lives because of sexual sin we give him another reason why he can block our healing.

The Book of Proverbs reveals that sexual immorality leads to something far deeper than we could ever imagine. Check out:

Proverbs 2:13-19 (NKJV): *From those who leave the paths of uprightness to walk in the ways of darkness; who rejoice in doing evil, and delight in the perversity of the wicked; whose ways are crooked, and who are devious in their paths; to deliver you from the immoral woman, from the seductress who flatters with her words, who forsakes the companion of her youth, and forgets the covenant of her God. <u>For her house leads down to death, and her paths to the dead; none who go to her return, nor do they regain the paths of life.</u>*

Proverbs 9:13-18 (NKJV): *The woman Folly is loud; she is seductive and knows nothing. She sits at the door of her house; she takes a seat on the highest places of the town, calling to those who pass by, who are going straight on their way, "Whoever is simple, let him turn in here!" And to him who lacks sense she says, "Stolen water is sweet, and bread eaten in secret is pleasant." But he does not know that the dead are there, that her guests are in the depths of Sheol.*

The depths of Sheol, otherwise referred in Scripture as the ungodly depth, the trap, the snare, the net, deep darkness etc. is a place inhabited by the Rephaim or dead ones (departed spirits).

(2) Sexual Victimization occurs when a male or female is sexually abused. Such abuse (rape, molestation etc.) is another way the enemy gains the legal right to hinder physical healing. Whether rape, molestation, or sexual harassment the enemy can block our healing when we refuse to forgive those who have victimized us. In Matthew 6:14-15 the Lord said:

For if you forgive others their trespasses, your heavenly Father will also forgive you, but if you do not forgive others their trespasses, neither will your Father forgive your trespasses. (ESV)

Forgiving someone who has abused you is not an easy decision to make, especially for those who have been abused by a family member. Worse, victims of sexual abuse often feel that they did something wrong and deserved to be abused, which causes them great shame and heartache.

A believer in her mid-twenties revealed to me that she had been molested by her cousin when she was a little girl. Ashamed and fearful, she decided not to tell anyone what had happened to her but changed her mind after visiting her OBGYN for a routine checkup. While there, she was triggered emotionally while being examined.

A small group of women and I huddled around her, broke soul ties with the cousin and called back all of her soul parts that had been entrapped in the ungodly depth and length. The friend that invited her to our service later reported that she was doing well.

Down through the years, I have ministered to both men and women who have been inappropriately touched during their childhood. Sadly, this horrific scheme of the enemy is all too common - the devil does not fight fair. He will employ any means that He can to entrap individuals in darkness, so they do not experience the abundance or fulfillment of God's plan and purpose for their lives.

For decades, Dylan Farrow alleged that her father Woody Allen sexually assaulted her in the attic of her mother Mia Farrow's Connecticut home on August 4, 1992. Only 7 at the time, Farrow stated in an interview on "CBS This Morning" the following account of what transpired. Whether it is true or not I do not know, but her testimony falls in line with the many stories I have heard from women who have been molested:

> We were in the TV room, and he reached behind me and touched my butt and then he told me to come up to the attic with him. I remember laying there on my stomach and my back was to him so I couldn't see what was going on. I felt trapped. He was saying things like we're gonna go to Paris together; you're gonna be in all my movies.
>
> Then he sexually assaulted me. I remember just focusing on my brother's train set and then he just stopped. He was done; and we just went downstairs. So... it's a very vulnerable (part) of me,

and a very... a very hurt (part) of me. There's a lot of... that little girl is in a lot of pain...

I very much hope that you listen to me with empathy, compassion and an open mind and heart and not use this as an opportunity to attack, turn away, criticize, mock; or shun "Little Dylan." This is the most vulnerable 'part' of who I am. I hope my sharing helps us find ways to allow painful secrets to come safely out of their closets so we all can heal and move forward in strength and peace. No longer ashamed, buried, scared, sad, and silent.

(3) Having an Abortion:

They sacrificed their sons and their daughters to the demons; they poured out innocent blood, the blood of their sons and daughters, whom they sacrificed to the idols of Canaan, and the land was polluted with blood. Thus they became unclean by their acts, and played the whore in their deeds. Then the anger of the Lord was kindled against his people, and he abhorred his heritage; he gave them into the hand of the nations, so that those who hated them ruled over them. Their enemies oppressed them, and they were brought into subjection under their power. Many times he delivered them, but they were rebellious in their purposes and were brought low through their iniquity. Psalm 106:37-43 (ESV)

Charlotte Dawson was a widely known and admired super model in both Australia and New Zealand. Dawson took her own life on February 22, 2014. Later, the cause of her tragic death came to light when the public learned that she fell into deep depression for 13 years after having had an abortion sometime between 1999 and the year 2000. She stated, "I don't know if a broken heart mends or learns to live in pieces."

This was an example of ungodly trading: Charlotte Dawson had an abortion because her husband, Scott Miller, convinced her that it was an inconvenient time to have a baby as he was trying out for the Australian Olympic swim. So, Charlotte obliged her husband and he drove her to an abortion clinic and dropped her off. As she left the clinic, she said that something inside of her shifted for the worse.

Like the Dawsons, many couples decide to abort their unborn children because the timing is not good for them. This is what I refer to as ungodly trading. In other words, couples trade their children's lives because it is either inconvenient, financially infeasible, or to protect their family's reputation from the stain of shame.

To my utter amazement, getting an abortion for some men and women is an easy decision. For others, it is gut wrenching! Either way, dealing with the emotional and spiritual consequences after an abortion is even harder and can last for a lifetime.

(4) Refusing to Forgive:
And do not grieve the Holy Spirit of God, by whom you were sealed for the day of redemption. Let all bitterness and wrath and anger and clamor and slander be put away from you, along with all malice. Be kind to one another, tenderhearted, forgiving one another, as God in Christ forgave you. Ephesians 4:30-32 (ESV)

Forgiveness is a choice. We can choose to forgive those who have wounded us, or we can choose not to forgive. But, because God has forgiven us for the many ways we have wounded Him, He expects us to follow His example.

Forgiving those who have hurt us, especially our close friends and loved ones, is easier said than done. If allowed to fester, unresolved anger and bitterness is a neon flashing sign that invites the enemy to take up residence in your soul. The key to overcoming bitterness, therefore, is to forgive quickly. If you don't exercise your will and take authority over your emotions, the enemy will thrust his poisoned-tip dagger into your heart and throw you in a prison cell. This is why I always ask an individual struggling to forgive someone who has deeply wounded them if there is even a small part of their heart that wants to forgive the person who hurt them. If they say, "Yes," I bless and encourage them to immediately exercise their will and give that part to Jesus. If you trust and obey the Lord by doing this, in time, He will heal your heart.

(5) Going to Bed Angry:

"Be angry, and do not sin": do not let the sun go down on your wrath, nor give place to the devil...Let all bitterness, wrath, anger, clamor, and evil speaking be put away from you, with all malice. And be kind to one another, tenderhearted, forgiving one another, even as God in Christ forgave you. Ephesians 4:26-27, 31-32 (NKJV)

The Greek word for place, territory, region, or opportunity is *topos*. When we go to bed without resolving our anger, we give the devil a *topos* to set up camp in our soul (mind, will and emotions). This is why my wife and I agreed early on in our marriage to never go to bed angry at one another without first forgiving and praying for each other. Over the years, we have maintained this commitment to one another even if it meant getting to bed at four AM.

(6) Making Blood Covenants:

You shall make no covenant with them and their gods. They shall not dwell in your land, lest they make you sin against me; for if you serve their gods, it will surely be a snare to you. Exodus 23:31-32 (ESV)

What is a 'blood covenant'? The Old Testament phrase literally means 'to cut a covenant'. This occurs when two people make a covenant with one another by cutting an incision on their wrists, joining hands, and lifting them to heaven in a promise.

Paul Cox has shed helpful light on his website regarding why blood covenants are established in the co-mingling of blood with other individuals is harmful, illustrating with his own personal experience.[1]

When we receive Jesus Christ as our personal savior His blood is appropriated to us, and a blood connection is formed between Jesus and us. Blood is important because "life is in the blood!" Therefore, any connection through any other blood is an ungodly connection. Only Jesus' perfect death on the cross and the shedding of His innocent blood can establish the blood covenant (connection) necessary to secure our salvation.

Making a blood covenant with a person is bad enough, but making a covenant established in blood with a false god is worse. In his book, H. Clay Trumbull, *The Blood Covenant*, H. Clay Trumbull sums up the danger of making blood pacts with false gods:

Because of God's spiritual laws, participation in the enemy's counterfeit systems puts a person into demonic bondage, and the blood covenants made with the demonic create curses that pass down through the generational lines.

There is power in blood sacrifice! This is why regularly remembering how Jesus spilled His blood to cleanse us from sin when we partake in the Lord's Supper is so powerful!

(7) Yoga and Dabbling in the Occult:
Do not turn to mediums or necromancers; do not seek them out, and so make yourselves unclean by them: I am the Lord your God. Leviticus 19:31 (ESV)

'Occult' means hidden, secret or supernatural, and is usually related to magical powers, such as witchcraft.

"Kundalini, come out!" When I heard these words spoken over me, I turned to the pastor who had prayed it and asked, "Why did you say that?" He replied, "I heard the Lord tell me to say it." Brand new to deliverance ministry, I was astounded because two years earlier I went to a chiropractor for an adjustment for a back injury. After receiving my treatment, he directed me to another room to get a massage from a woman on his staff. As she massaged my spine, up and down, she repeatedly invoked the name, Kundalini, and talked about chakra points. Naturally, I thought this was weird but was blind to the reality of what was transpiring in the spiritual realm and in my body.

So, when the pastor called out, "Kundalini, come out!" I was shocked, and then to my utter surprise I began to writhe in severe pain as the spirit manifested in my spine. According to Wikipedia, 'Kundalini' is the term for a spiritual energy or life force located at the base of the spine, conceptualized as a coiled-up serpent. The practice of Kundalini yoga is supposed to arouse the sleeping Kundalini Shakti from its coiled base, through the 6 chakras and penetrate the 7th chakra, or crown (a chakra is an energy point on the body).

Let's get back to the rest of my story. After writhing in terrible pain for 15 minutes, the spirit of Kundalini finally left me. I was flabbergasted! "How could a demon be in me?" After all, I was a Southern Baptist pastor. I was not only shocked; I was embarrassed! It was my wake-up call about the reality of the spiritual realm.

As I reflect now on my surprising introduction to deliverance ministry, I must say how incredibly grateful I am unto the Lord. I say this because for the last twenty-seven years, my back has been free of the severe pain that I had endured for years after getting treated by my New Age chiropractor.

If you are a Yoga practitioner my heart is not to condemn you, but rather to inform you of its' dangers by sharing what happened to me. Obviously, I did not practice Yoga, but my chiropractor and his masseuse did. Out of ignorance I allowed my chiropractor's masseuse to place her hands on me while she spoke about chakras, not knowing that I was opening myself up to demonic infiltration.

Spiritism is the belief that the dead communicate with the living. A strong Christian male in our church family shared with me that he grew up in a New York City home with a mother and grandmother who practiced Santeria, a religion that began in West Africa and the Caribbean in which the worship of the dead or departed spirits is regularly practiced. During his childhood, this man saw spiritual phenomena like open coffins with the dead inside, snakes slithering on the floor, and other frightening images that were burned into his mind in his home. He eventually left New York and came to Hawaii where he became a Christian. Several years ago, he repented and renounced the practice of Santeria in his maternal family line and is thriving today!

So, here's the deal. If you dabble in the occult, you will give the devil a wide-open opportunity to enter your body and soul, which will result in demonization, nightmares, frightening visions and other paranormal activity.

(8) Making Inner Vows (Computer Programs of the Soul):
And I will give you a new heart, and a new spirit I will put within you. And I will remove the heart of stone from your flesh and give you a heart of flesh.
Ezekiel 36:26 (ESV)

A heart of stone is a wall of protection that an individual consciously and unconsciously builds around their heart to prevent ever being hurt or disappointed again. Such was the case of a woman who was a part of our church family for several years. Raised by a father who had experienced wartime violence, she endured her father's angry outbursts for most of her childhood.

During a ministry session I inquired if she had had a sense of belonging while growing up. She replied, "No." Her motivation for seeing me was linked to several very caring friends who had lovingly pointed out to her that she went from church to church, never putting down roots in any one family of believers. She shared that her desire was to deal with this pattern and, in time, plant herself in a church long term.

In response to what she shared, it was obvious to me that because she feared her dad's outbursts and subsequent punishment that she had walled off her heart to 'never to belong' to a church family lest she be disappointed like she had been over and over during her childhood.

1 John 4:18 (NKJV) proclaims: *"There is no fear in love; but perfect love casts out fear, because fear involves torment. But he who fears has not been made perfect in love."*

In the KJV version of 1 John 4:18, Jesus said that He would not leave us comfortless or as orphans. The orphan stronghold is a dysfunctional mindset rooted in fear, hopelessness and the absence or abuse of love. We are all, in some way, wounded to love because we have all been parented by imperfect parents.

Orphan mindsets are downloaded into us like computer programs when we consciously or unconsciously vow or promise ourselves not to be hurt or disappointed again. The woman described above promised herself not to be a part of any family for the fear of eventually being rejected, disappointed, or punished. Once abused or traumatized like she was, children are especially vulnerable to the lies of the enemy and silently build a wall of self-protection around their hearts to destroy basic trust with others.

(9) Adverse Childhood Experiences:
According to Dr. Robert Black, the former president of the American Academy of Pediatrics, "Adverse childhood experiences are the single greatest unaddressed health threat facing our nation today."

By definition, an Adverse Childhood Experience, or ACE, is a traumatic childhood event that has a negative, long-lasting effect on an individual's physical health and emotional well-being. These include adverse experiences such as:

- Watching a parent regularly abuse alcohol and drugs
- The premature death of a parent before the age of 18
- Being raised by a parent who was hyper-religious
- Being raised by a parent who was mentally ill
- Being physically, verbally or sexually abused
- Not having enough, food, clothing or shelter
- Being raised by a parent who had PTSD
- Not feeling loved or special
- An incarcerated parent
- Divorce or separation

According the cdc.gov website, 61% of adults in America have had at least one ACE and 16% have had 4 or more types of ACEs. Those who have had at least 4 ACEs are:

- 2 times more likely to develop liver disease
- 3 times more likely to develop lung disease as the result of smoking
- 4 times more likely to start having sex by the age of 15
- 4.5 times more likely to develop depression
- 11 times more likely to be an IV drug user

Many people are not aware of the correlation between having multiple adverse childhood experiences and health issues across the lifespan. Shockingly, at least 5 out the top 10 leading causes of death in the United States today are associated with ACEs. And more surprisingly, those adults who have had 6 or more ACEs are more likely to die prematurely than those who have had none.

So, here's my million-dollar question? What is the enemy's end game when he traumatizes a child? To answer this question, I recommend that you re-read Genesis chapter three in its entirety. This chapter if you recall reveals how Adam and Eve lived in the Garden of Eden basking in the security and protection of their Father's embrace until they were seduced by the *nacash* (the shining one/snake) and ate from the tree of knowledge of good and evil. In an instant Adam and Eve were devoid of their Father's comfort; and fear, stress and anxiety entered in:

> *And they heard the sound of the Lord God walking in the garden in the cool of the day, and the man and his wife hid themselves from the presence of the Lord God among the trees of the garden. So when the woman saw that the tree was good for food, and that it was a delight to the eyes, and that the tree was to be desired to make one wise, she took of its fruit and ate, and she also gave some to her husband who was with her, and he ate. Then the eyes of both were opened, and they knew that they were naked. And they sewed fig leaves together and made themselves loincloths. Genesis 3:6-8 (ESV)*

Once secure, the first couple hid in fear behind the trees. All of us deal with fear, stress, or anxiety to some extent. Because of the Fall we are prone to fear. We fret over our families, our social relationships, our health, our finances, and our careers. Children are especially susceptible to fear. Knowing this the enemy strategically bombards them with fear and anxiety when their parents argue, use drugs, abuse them etc.

So once again, what's the enemy's end game? It's to flood a child's bloodstream with a hormone called cortisol at the cellular and sub cellular levels so that later as an adult their capacity to serve the Lord is limited or worse. This raises the question, "What is cortisol?" According to WebMD cortisol is nature's built-in alarm system or your body's main stress hormone.

The Cleveland Clinic lists three primary types of stress:

- Acute
- Chronic
- Traumatic

Acute stress floods your bloodstream when you experience an unexpected event like your boss yelling at you, or nearly being hit by a car out on the freeway. Chronic stress is normally tied to long-term situations that are pressure packed such as having to care daily for an aging parent with Alzheimer's or dealing with a debilitating condition in your own life. Traumatic stress affects your body when you experience a life-threatening, abusive, or dangerous situation that causes you to feel afraid and absolutely helpless like being molested or raped.

Matthew Solon, the Execute Editor, of the Harvard Men's Health Watch wrote a short article entitled, *Prolonged Stress May Increase the Risk of Death From Cancer,* saying:

> Long-term exposure to stress has long been known to increase risk for cardiovascular disease. A study in the September 2022 issue of SSM—Population Health suggests it also may raise the risk of dying from cancer…

The connection between stress and cancer could be related to the body's exposure to cortisol, the stress hormone. The body releases cortisol during stressful events, but levels usually decrease once the threat has passed. However, exposure to ongoing stressors can keep cortisol levels consistently high, which can wear down the body on a cellular level, according to the research team. They added that other studies have suggested this reaction may raise the risk of cancer or cause existing cancer to spread more rapidly.

If you have had several ACEs I encourage you to deal squarely and courageously with them via a skillful prayer counselor so that your cells are cleansed of fear by the love of God:

> *There is no fear in love, but perfect love casts out fear. For fear has to do with punishment, and whoever fears has not been perfected in love. 1 John 4:18 (ESV)*

(10) Generational Sin:
> *You shall not make for yourself a carved image, or any likeness of anything that is in heaven above, or that is on the earth beneath, or that is in the water under the earth. You shall not bow down to them or serve them; for I the Lord your God am a jealous God, visiting the iniquity of the fathers on the children to the third and fourth generation of those who hate me, but showing steadfast love to thousands of those who love me and keep my commandments. Deuteronomy 5:8-10 (ESV)*

In the November 2000, I traveled to Buenos Aires, Argentina to attend a conference hosted by Ed Silvoso and Harvest Evangelism. While there I attended a workshop taught by Paul Cox.

Two months later Paul and his wife Donna were invited to Oahu, Hawaii by Cal Chinen. Paul was to do generational deliverance prayer ministry over pastors on Oahu. Each of the pastors were scheduled to meet with him and were told to be aware of any dreams they had before the meeting.

The next day, my wife Barbara and I met Paul for the first time. After a brief introduction, he asked me if I had had a dream. I replied yes and shared that in the dream I saw four men standing side by side outside a brothel in Japan. Paul then asked me if I was Japanese, and I said that my mother was 100% Japanese. Paul then remarked, "Your dream indicates that the stronghold of sexual immorality is flowing down to you from four generations back on your mother's side of the family." He then shocked me as he looked into my eyes and inquired, "Rob, have you ever committed adultery?" With my wife at my side I said, "No." But, what I forgot to tell Paul at the time was that between the age of 12 and 24 I had been hooked on pornography. If you're wondering about what happened during my prayer session, Paul asked the Lord to break all generational ties between me and the stronghold of sexual immorality.

The above account was my introduction to the power and effectiveness of generational prayer deliverance ministry. In case you're wondering, I had been delivered a year earlier from pornography through a fellow pastor on Oahu but was not aware of the reality of generational strongholds. I wonder today if Christian leaders who have had to step down because of sexual sin in recent years had gone through generational deliverance, they would still be in ministry today? Only God knows, but my point in bringing this up is to open your eyes to the reality or existence of demonic strongholds rooted in your family line.

A Shocking Manifestation:

After getting delivered of multiple strongholds in the 90's I began to learn how to deliver the demonized. During an afternoon class in 2002 that was attended by about 40 people, I discerned that the Lord wanted to heal someone of arthritis. I asked those present if anyone had struggled with arthritis and a woman in her 40's raised her hand. I then asked if she had been struggling to forgive someone from a past hurt or if someone in her family line was struggling with the same issue. She responded by saying that both her mother and grandmother dealt with this issue.

After leading this woman to forgive her mother and grandmother. I broke generational ties between them. Instantly, the woman began to shriek at the top of her lungs as the Holy Spirit began to flush the generational spirit of arthritis out of her hand. To the utter amazement of everyone present, the woman's arm, forearm and hand began to twist causing the woman to scream in great pain. This manifestation went on for two long minutes and then the woman's entire limb went limp.

Ten years later I met this woman and asked her if the Lord had healed her of arthritis. To my joy she told me that she had been arthritis free ever since! Satan and his demonic horde can infiltrate our thoughts, emotions and physical bodies through the sinful choices we make, the trauma inflicted upon us by others and through the sins of our ancestors.

Now that we have learned some of the ways the enemy gains legal access into our lives, I'd like to address in Chapter Two why the church is lacking the divine power today to unseat the enemy from our lives.

---

[1] https://aslansplace.com/language/en/the-blood-covenant-paul-l-cox/

CHAPTER TWO:

POWER OUTAGE

ROB GROSS

I Want My Church Back:
Then Jesus returned <u>in the power of the</u> Spirit to Galilee, and news of Him went out through all the surrounding region. And He taught in their synagogues, being glorified by all... When the sun was setting, all those who had any that were sick with various diseases brought them to Him; and He laid His hands on every one of them and healed them. Luke 4:14-15, 40 (NKJV)

In 1993 I attended my denomination's annual conference on the island of Maui which began on a Friday evening. To everyone's dismay the power in the hotel, where the conference was being held, went out. Hotel management tried to get the power turned back on but were unsuccessful. As I sat in the dark the Holy Spirit whispered to me, "This power outage is a symbol of the powerlessness in the church." Without lighting we were excused to our rooms.

The next morning all the conference attendees were informed that the conference was canceled because the hotel was unable to turn the power on. I hopped on a plane and returned to Oahu.

The Gospels clearly state that power undergirded the ministry of Jesus. Such was the case in Luke 5: 17-24 (NKJV):

Now it happened on a certain day, as He was teaching, that there were Pharisees and teachers of the law sitting by, who had come out of every town of Galilee, Judea, and Jerusalem. And the power of the Lord was present to heal them. Then behold, men brought on a bed a man who was paralyzed, whom they sought to bring in and lay before Him. And when they could not find how they might bring him in, because of the crowd, they went up on the housetop and let him down with his bed through the tiling into the midst before Jesus. When He saw their faith, He said to him, "Man, your sins are forgiven you." Immediately he rose up before them, took up what he had been lying on, and departed to his own house, glorifying God.

And they were all amazed, and they glorified God and were filled with fear, saying, "We have seen strange things today!" And the scribes and the Pharisees began to reason, saying, "Who is this who speaks blasphemies? Who can forgive sins but God alone?" But when Jesus perceived their thoughts, He answered and said to them, "Why are you reasoning in your hearts? Which is easier, to say, 'Your sins are forgiven you,' or to say, 'Rise up and walk'? But that you may know that **the Son of Man has power** on earth to forgive sins" — He said to the man who was paralyzed, "I say to you, arise, take up your bed, and go to your house."

Before Jesus ascended into heaven, He said on two different occasions that His disciples would receive power:

"Behold, I send the Promise of My Father upon you; but tarry in the city of Jerusalem until you are endued with power from on high." Luke 24:49 (NKJV)

"But you shall receive power when the Holy Spirit has come upon you; and you shall be witnesses to

Me in Jerusalem, and in all Judea and Samaria, and to the end of the earth." Acts 1:8 (NKJV)

These statements by the Lord lead me to raise the question, "Where is the power of the Lord to heal the sick and bind up the brokenhearted in the church today?" Now I'm not saying that the power of the Holy Spirit is not present today altogether throughout the Church, but I am saying that the power of God is not flowing yet on a widespread basis.

In John 14:12, Jesus made an astounding statement that the church would do greater works than He did. Where is the evidence of this in the earth today? Once again, I believe that the greater works of Jesus are being affected in small pockets around the globe, but in general are few and far between.

God Wants to Turn the Power Back On:
In 1996, while attending an evening service at the Winds of Revival conference at First Assembly of God in Honolulu, I listened to Roger Helland say that the power of God was a non-factor in the church. As soon as Helland uttered these words the power in the auditorium went off just like it had in Maui three years prior. Helland proceeded to share that it was the Lord's intention to turn the power of God back on in the church. Just as the power had gone off earlier the power in the room went back on. Everyone in the room that night got the message the Lord was trying to convey.

This leads to a third question, "Why is there a power outage in the church today? I would like to suggest several reasons:

1. **Religiosity**

> *For I desire mercy and not sacrifice, and the knowledge of God more than burnt offerings.* Hosea 6:6 (NKJV)

Throughout Matthew, Mark and Luke, Jesus cast out many demons. A closer look at the Gospel of John, however, reveals no mention of Jesus casting out a single demon. Why, you may ask? Although Jesus did not cast out any demons in the Gospel of John, He was constantly battling the scribes and Pharisees or the religious spirit. According to 2 Timothy 3:1-5 the primary assignment of the religious spirit is to have the church "maintain an outward form of godliness", while denying the power and works of the Holy Spirit. This spiritual assignment can be seen at work in the following passages:

> *They went each to his own house, but Jesus went to the Mount of Olives. Early in the morning he came again to the temple. All the people came to him, and he sat down and taught them. <u>The scribes and the Pharisees</u> brought a woman who had been caught in adultery, and placing her in the midst they said to him, "Teacher, this woman has been caught in the act of adultery. Now in the Law, Moses commanded us to stone such women. So what do you say?" This they said to test him, that they might have some charge to bring against him. Jesus bent down and wrote with his finger on the ground. And as they continued to ask him, he stood up and said to them, "Let him who is without sin among you be the first to throw a stone at her." And once more he bent down and wrote on the ground. But when they heard it, they went away one by one, beginning with the older ones, and Jesus was left alone with the woman standing before him. Jesus stood up and said to her, "Woman, where are they?*

Has no one condemned you?" She said, "No one, Lord." And Jesus said, "Neither do I condemn you; go, and from now on sin no more." John 8:1-11 (ESV)

<u>They brought to the Pharisees</u> the man who had formerly been blind. Now it was a Sabbath day when Jesus made the mud and opened his eyes. So <u>the Pharisees</u> again asked him how he had received his sight. And he said to them, "He put mud on my eyes, and I washed, and I see." <u>Some of the Pharisees</u> said, "This man is not from God, for he does not keep the Sabbath." John 9:14-16 (ESV)

At that time the Feast of Dedication took place at Jerusalem. It was winter, and Jesus was walking in the temple, in the colonnade of Solomon. So the Jews gathered around him and said to him, "How long will you keep us in suspense? If you are the Christ, tell us plainly." Jesus answered them, "I told you, and you do not believe. The works that I do in my Father's name bear witness about me, but you do not believe because you are not among my sheep. I give them eternal life, and they will never perish, and no one will snatch them out of my hand. My Father, who has given them to me, is greater than all, and no one is able to snatch them out of the Father's hand. <u>The Jews</u> picked up stones again to stone him. Jesus answered them, "I have shown you many good works from the Father; for which of them are you going to stone me?" <u>The Jews</u> answered him, "It is not for a good work that we are going to stone you but for blasphemy, because you, being a man, make yourself God." Jesus answered them, "Is it not written in your Law, 'I said, you are gods'? If he called them gods to whom the word of God came—and Scripture cannot be *broken— do you say of him whom the Father consecrated and sent into the world, 'You are blaspheming,' because I said, 'I am the Son of God'? but if I do them, even though you do not believe me, believe the works, that you may know and understand that the Father is in me and I am in the Father." Again they sought to arrest him, but he escaped from their hands. John 10:22-39 (ESV)*

The Gospel adds another example of the religious spirit in action:

But if you had known what means, 'I desire mercy and not sacrifice,' you would not have condemned the guiltless. For the Son of Man is Lord even of the Sabbath." Now when He had departed from there, He went into their synagogue. And behold, there was a man who had a withered hand. And they asked Him, saying, "Is it lawful to heal on the Sabbath?" — that they might accuse Him. Then He said to them, "What man is there among you who has one sheep, and if it falls into a pit on the Sabbath, will not lay hold of it and lift out? Of how much more value then is a man than a sheep? Therefore it is lawful to do good on the Sabbath." Then He said to the man, "Stretch out your hand." And he stretched it out, and it was restored as whole as the other. Then the Pharisees went out and plotted against Him, how they might destroy Him. Matthew 12:7-14 (NKJV)

When the Spirit of God began to flow in our small Baptist church in the mid 1990's the religious spirit attempted to stop what the Lord was birthing when a visiting missionary veered from his message about missions and began to speak against the baptism of the Holy Spirit. Concerned that the enemy was trying to snuff out the move of the Spirit I stood up and asked him to leave. Yup, I asked him to leave in the middle of his message. Many in the congregation were relieved and thanked me later, but our number one giver was offended and showed up at my home the next day to say that she and her husband were leaving the church.

In his book, "Exposing the Religious Spirit" Jack Deere lists 15 characteristics of the religious spirit. Numbers 12 and 15 explain why some pastors, leaders and church members in the corporate church of Christ are opposed to the power of the Holy Spirit:

> 12) **RESISTANT** – A religious person will tend to resist the supernatural or reject spiritual manifestations he or she cannot understand.

> 15) **REFRAIN** – Someone religious will tend to be suspicious of or even oppose new moves of God.

So, here's the deal. A leader who is spiritually influenced by a religious spirit will gravitate towards legalism (the form of godliness without the power) and vehemently accuse the work of the Holy Spirit as the work of the devil. Why? Because the Holy Spirit sets people free to love God and serve His cause passionately (fulfill the Great Commission). In sum, the devil is not threatened if the Body of Christ plays church, but if the family of Jesus is open to the Father's power the enemy will rise up.

2. Baby Formula Instead of the Breast

So Jesus said, "I speak to you eternal truth. The Son is unable to do anything from himself or through his own initiative. I only do the works that I see the

Father doing, for the Son does the same works as his Father." John 5:19 (TPT)

Baby formula is a scientifically manufactured milk mixture or 'substitute' for breast milk. Did you get that? Baby formula is not the real deal! It's an imitation. The advantages of formula feeding are the connivence and flexibility it provides for busy moms, while the major disadvantages are the lack of anti-bodies that build up a newborn's immune system and the lack of skin-to-skin contact between a mother and her child.

One of my favorite names for God is El Shaddai. The word 'Shaddai' is derived from 'shad' meaning breast. While most Bible translators render El Shaddai as 'God Almighty', the name El Shaddai also means the 'many breasted one.' Given the current powerless ness in the church, we must ask ourselves if our churches are formula focused (our programs) or are they presence focused (skin-to-skin connection at God's breast)?

According to John 5:19 Jesus could do nothing except what He 'saw' His Father doing. The success of His ministry was not based on a prescribed formula of rules, but on what He discerned His Father was doing. As mentioned above in John 8, Jesus rescued a woman caught in adultery. As her accusers sought His take on the matter He bent down and wrote with His finger something on the ground. What was Jesus up to? I think He was zeroing in on what His Father was doing and how He wanted Him to respond. Perhaps Jesus asked, "Father, what are You doing?" And the Father responded, "I am releasing the revelation of grace to My people. At present they are religiously focused on the letter of the Law instead of the heart of the Law. Tell them that he who has no sin, cast the first stone." The letter of the Law or formula stated, "Stone the adulterer", but the heart of the

Law said, "Woman, where are your accusers? Go and sin no more."

According to Miriam-Webster's dictionary the word 'formula' has multiple definitions including, "A customary or set form or method allowing little room for originality." Based on John 8 we could add, "A customary or set form or method allowing little room for grace."

Programmatic designed, seeker sensitive and purpose driven churches shaped American church culture in the 1980's and 90's, drawing large numbers of 'seekers' into the church. These churches catered to the needs of pre-believers offering short worship services and 'how to' messages. This wineskin allowed pre-believers to check out the Gospel at their own pace without religious requirements. Although effective in drawing the Lost to their weekend services, seeker sensitive churches did not give room for the power of the Holy Spirit to confront the powers of darkness that held seekers captive.

With every second of their services timed to near perfection there was no room for Jesus to move accordingly. In addition, with every service planned out in advance the enemy knew exactly what to expect on any given weekend.

Are We Moving with the Cloud or the Program?
And the Lord went before them by day in a pillar of cloud to lead the way, and by night in a pillar of fire to give them light, so as to go by day and night.
Exodus 13:21 (NKJV)

When our weekend services and programs supersede the leadership of the Holy Spirit we are moving in our own strength and wisdom leaving no room for God to move. When the Israelites wandered in the wilderness for 40 years

God led them by the pillar of cloud by day and the pillar of fire by night meaning that they did not move from place to place unless the Lord moved first.

Several years ago, I was invited to minister healing at a seeker sensitive church. When I arrived at the church facility, I was introduced to the pastor who informed me that I had 3 minutes to share. At first, I was taken aback, but wanting to serve the church I complied. While waiting upfront to go on stage I sat next to a young woman with a headset on her head. Right before walking on stage, she turned to me and said, "The senior pastor just called and informed me that He's giving you four more minutes to speak (I had been invited to share about divine healing)."

After the service, I was told that the extra 4 minutes I was given was highly unusual. The person who had invited me to speak was upset about this, but I wasn't because I knew that this was the way their church rolled (they were a seeker sensitive congregation). I'm happy to report that in-spite of the time constraints, the Lord still healed two people that night!

> *And the Lord went before them by day in a pillar of cloud to lead the way, and by night in a pillar of fire to give them light, so as to go by day and night.*
> *Exodus 13:21 (NKJV)*

Chronos Versus Kairos Time:
In the Western church we are on the clock. We worship the Lord for 25 minutes, share announcements for upcoming events for 5 minutes, hear someone share a testimony for 10 minutes and listen to the morning message for 40 minutes and then we're out the door.

One might say that in America we are slaves to time. According to whippet.org the ancient Greeks had two words for time. The first was *chronos,* which we still use in words like chronological and anachronism. It refers to clock time — time that can be measured — seconds, minutes, hours, years. Where *chronos* is quantitative, kairos is qualitative. It measures moments, not seconds. It refers to the right moment, the opportune moment. The perfect moment such as when a mother gives birth to her child.

The above definitions beg the question, "If our services are operating on *chronos,* where does this leave time for the Lord to do or say what He wants to do or say? How many divine breakthroughs have we aborted because we have not allowed for the Holy Spirit to move in our service because of the constraints of *chronos*?

3. Not Inquiring of the Lord

Now when the Philistines heard that they had anointed David king over Israel, all the Philistines went up to search for David. And David heard of it and went down to the stronghold. The Philistines also went and deployed themselves in the Valley of Rephaim. So David inquired of the Lord, saying, "Shall I go up against the Philistines? Will You deliver them into my hand?" And the Lord said to David, "Go up, for I will doubtless deliver the Philistines into your hand." So David went to Baal Perazim, and David defeated them there; and he said, "The Lord has broken through my enemies before me, like a breakthrough of water." Therefore he called the name of that place Baal Perazim. And they left their images there, and David and his men carried them away. Therefore David inquired of the Lord, and He said, "You shall not go up; circle around behind them, and come upon them in front of the mulberry trees. Then the Philistines went up once again and deployed themselves in the Valley of Rephaim. And it shall be, when you hear the sound of marching in the tops of the mulberry trees, then you shall advance quickly. For then the Lord will go out before you to strike the camp of the Philistines." And David did so, as the Lord commanded him; and he drove back the Philistines from Geba as far as Gezer. 2 Samuel 5:17-25 (NKJV)

God moved in power on David's behalf because David asked Him first what to do instead of moving forward in his own strength and wisdom. Could it be that we have limited the power of God to flow in our gatherings because we have failed to A.T.L. (Ask the Lord) what He wants to do?

4. The of Fear Man

Proverbs 29:25 warns us that the fear of man is a snare or trap. When I began to follow the leading of the Holy Spirit, as opposed to a seeker sensitive platform, I had to consider two scenarios or questions: 1) How would I deal with those in our congregation who were accustomed to a seeker sensitive, purpose driven service and 2) How would I deal with those who I knew were opposed to Holy Spirit manifestations?

Thinking about these questions sent shivers down my spine because I feared that people would leave the church and diminish our ability to, 'pay the bills'. I tried my best to appease both groups, but 30 people still left the church, unwilling to support the new move of God. Looking back, I now realize that there was nothing I could have done to stop the Lord from clearing His house of those who did not understand what He was doing.

By fallen nature we are creatures of fear. The moment Adam and Eve ate from the tree of knowledge of good and evil they became fearful beings hindering their ability to trust their once Heavenly Father. Genesis 3:6-10 (NKJV) paints the picture:

> *So when the woman saw that the tree was good for food, that it was pleasant to the eyes, and a tree desirable to make one wise, she took of its fruit and ate. She also gave to her husband with her, and he ate. Then the eyes of both of them were opened, and they knew that they were naked; and they sewed fig leaves together and made themselves coverings. And they heard the sound of the Lord God walking in the garden in the cool of the day, and Adam and his wife hid themselves from the presence of the Lord God among the trees of the garden. Then the Lord God called to Adam and said to him, "Where are you?" So he said, "I heard Your voice in the garden, and I was afraid because I was naked; and I hid myself.*

Filled with fear from the Fall, we are afraid of what others think and say about us (i.e., 'Cancel Culture'). After I renounced the fear of man, I was able to invite the power of the Holy Spirit to invade our meetings. It was the best decision I've ever made!

If you are presently struggling with the fear of man, memorize what Paul said to Timothy in 2 Timothy 1:7 :

> *For God has not given us a spirit of fear, but of power and of love and of a sound mind. (NKJV)*

5. The Fallacy of Being in Control

Trust in the Lord with all your heart, and do not lean on your own understanding. In all your ways acknowledge him, and he will make straight your paths. Proverbs 3:5-6 (ESV)

A fallacy is defined as a mistaken belief, especially one based on an unsound argument.

We have all, at one time or another, believed the fallacy that we're in control. The reality is that none of us have ever been in control of the events, circumstances or people that surround us. Yes, we can exercise self-control, but that's it. We either give control to God by faith or we give control to the wicked one by acting upon the fallacy that we are in control.

One of the major reasons why there is such a power outage in the church today is because God's gatekeepers have refused to give over control of God's house to God. I agree that church programs keep things orderly, but when they do not give room for the Holy Spirit to move they shut down the heavenly power grid.

I Want My Church Back!
In 1996, while at First Assembly of God Red Hill with a group of gatekeepers (pastors and leaders), I fell to the floor under the power of God. As the Holy Spirit filled my entire being I began to weep profusely and repeatedly cried out, "I want My church back, I want my church back! Why won't you give her back to Me?" Engulfed by God's fiery presence I then began to prophesy that the wind of God's Spirit would sweep across the Hawaiian Islands and tens of thousands of the unsaved would be swept into the kingdom of God.

If we want to see a reformational shift of the Spirit in the church, God's gatekeepers must be willing to give back control to the Holy Spirit.

Prior to being encountered by the Lord in 1996 while at First Assembly of God, I had a vivid dream of a 900-foot wave hurtling towards Oahu's southern shore. As I watched this enormous wave crest, I saw hundreds of believers standing on a wall watching the wave come toward them. Then to my horror and surprise the wave crashed over the wall and swept every believer to their death below including my wife. I wept crying, "My bride, my bride, my precious bride!"

As I have reflected about the meaning of this dream over the years, I have concluded that it was about the coming (and now ongoing) reformation of the church and its structures that have kept it from moving in the power of the Acts church. This reformation will uproot the religiosity and control in the Body of Christ that has been opposed to the power of God. Many believers will resist the new move of God while others will embrace it and walk in kingdom power.

6. Aborted Ideas and Solutions from Heaven

There are six things that the Lord hates, seven that are an abomination to him: haughty eyes, a lying tongue, and hands that shed innocent blood, a heart that devises wicked plans, feet that make haste to run to evil, a false witness who breathes out lies, and one who sows discord among brothers. Proverbs 6:16-19 (ESV)

It was 1978, and my girlfriend at the time (not my wife) informed me that she was pregnant. Not wanting to face our parents or be parents ourselves, we decided to get an abortion. Although I know the Lord has fully forgiven me (and I have forgiven myself), I deeply regret taking my unborn child's life.

Abortion is a form of ungodly trading. Like my girlfriend and I, people trade their children's lives for convenience, or concern over their finances and protecting their family's reputation. Once the transaction is finalized, guilt, shame and self-condemnation drop like a hammer. Such was the case when a woman in her 40's met with me at my office in 1998. She sat down and placed on the table between us several syringes (she was hooked on heroin). When I asked her what heroin did for her, she shared that it eased the pain of having had six abortions. I asked her if I could pray for her, and she consented. What followed was shocking as she began to wail under the power of God crying, "My babies, my babies, my babies!"

According to the World Health Organization, every year in the world there are around <u>73 million induced abortions</u>. This corresponds to approximately 200,000 abortions per day.

According to the Guttmacher Institute since the inception of Roe vs Wade in 1973 there have 63,459,781 abortions in America alone.

In the USA, where nearly 30% of pregnancies are unintended and 40% of these are terminated by abortion, there are between 1,500 to 2,500 abortions per day. Nearly 20% of all pregnancies in the USA (excluding miscarriages) end in abortion. Guttmacher Institute reports 930,160 abortions performed in 2020 in the United States, with a rate of 14.4 per 1,000 women.

Note: There are two basic sources on abortion data in the U.S.: The U.S. Centers for Disease Control (CDC) publishes yearly but relies on voluntary reports from state health departments (and New York City, Washington, D.C.). The Guttmacher Institute contacts abortion clinics directly for data but does not survey every year.

The Cost of Aborting 63 Million Babies:
Paul Cox called me and said, "Rob, I think I just heard something profound from the Lord." "What did He say?" "I think I heard Him say that one of the major reasons why we haven't seen more people get healed in America today is because the divine solutions for the diseases people are facing today were rooted in the 63 million babies aborted since 1973."

Judges 9:5 (ESV):

> *And he went to his father's house at Ophrah and killed his brothers the sons of Jerubbaal, seventy men, on one stone. But Jotham the youngest son of Jerubbaal was left, for he hid himself.*

By eliminating most of his 70 half-brothers (except Jotham), Abimelech usurped the leadership of his father's (Gideon's) clan. 69 lives were lost on that terrible day, but the loss was far more than physical. By murdering his brothers Abimelech removed 69 unique gifts, wirings and callings that could have been a blessing to the tribe of Gideon and beyond. By aborting 63 million fetuses (since the passage of Roe vs Wade) we have eliminated millions of potential medical inventions, remedies, formulas and solutions for the wide spectrum of physical and emotional ills facing our society today. Forgive us Lord Jesus for this terrible sin and the wanton waste of human resources.

7. Sexual Immorality in the Church

Sex outside of marriage, as I mentioned in Chapter One, gives the enemy the legal right to slime us with toxic waste. When sexual immorality is openly accepted in the church it leads to severe consequences and siphon's away the power we need to set others free from demonic captivity. The following passages from 1 Samuel 2-4 makes this vividly clear:

> *Now Eli was very old; and he heard everything his sons did to all Israel, and how they lay with the women who assembled at the door of the tabernacle of meeting. So he said to them, "Why do you do such things? For I hear of your evil dealings from all the people. No, my sons! For it is not a good report that I hear. You make the Lord's people transgress. If one man sins against another, God will judge him. But if a man sins against the Lord, who will intercede for him?" Nevertheless they did not heed the voice of their father, because the Lord desired to kill them. 1 Samuel 2:22-25 (NASB)*

> *For I have told him that I will judge his house forever for the iniquity which he knows, because his sons made themselves vile, and he did not restrain them. In that day I will perform against Eli all that I have spoken concerning his house, from beginning to end. Then the Lord said to Samuel: "Behold, I will do something in Israel at which both ears of everyone who hears it will tingle. And therefore I have sworn to the house of Eli that the iniquity of Eli's house shall not be atoned for by sacrifice or offering forever." 1 Samuel 3:11-14 (NASB)*

> *Now his (Samuel's) daughter-in-law, Phinehas' wife, was pregnant and about to give birth; and*

when she heard the news that the ark of God had been taken and that her father-in-law and her husband had died, she kneeled down and gave birth, because her pains came upon her. When he mentioned the ark of God, Eli fell off the seat backward beside the gate, and his neck was broken and he died, for he was old and heavy. And so he judged Israel for forty years. And about the time of her death the women who were standing by her said to her, "Do not be afraid, for you have given birth to a son." But she did not answer or pay attention. And she named the boy Ichabod, saying, "The glory has departed from Israel," because the ark of God had been taken and because of her father-in-law and her husband. So she said, "The glory has departed from Israel, because the ark of God has been taken." 1 Samuel 4:18-22 (NASB)

A Stern Warning:

Prior to entering the land of Canaan, the Lord issued a stern warning to Moses and the people of Israel saying in Leviticus 18:25-28 (NKJV):

Do not defile yourselves with any of these things; for by all these the nations are defiled, which I am casting out before you. For the land is defiled; therefore I visit the punishment of its iniquity upon it, and the land vomits out its inhabitants. You shall therefore keep My statutes and My judgments, and shall not commit any of these abominations, either any of your own nation or any stranger who dwells among you (for all these abominations the men of the land have done, who were before you, and thus the land is defiled), lest the land vomit you out also when you defile it, as it vomited out the nations that were before you.

What did the Lord mean when He said, "Do not defile yourselves with any of these things?" The answer precedes the above quote in Leviticus 18:20-23:

> *And you shall not lie sexually with your neighbor's wife and so make yourself unclean with her. You shall not give any of your children to offer them to Molech, and so profane the name of your God: I am the Lord. You shall not lie with a male as with a woman; it is an abomination. And you shall not lie with any animal and so make yourself unclean with it, neither shall any woman give herself to an animal to lie with it: it is perversion.*

The consequence of sex outside of marriage and child sacrifice as it pertains to a land area, region or nation is not on our radar screen. The land where we live will issue us a divorce decree or spit (vomit) us out when sexual sin and abortion is rampant.

A Divorce Decree:
What does 'vomited or spit out', mean? It is to reject or, in essence, issue us a divine divorce decree; making it challenging, if not impossible, for us to put down our roots in a land area and experience the multiplied blessings of the Lord. How does the land reject us? Through natural disasters (i.e., hurricanes, floods, fires, tornadoes), unemployment, violence, crime, homelessness, and unsecured borders. When God is in covenant with the people of a land area and the people keep His covenant, the land will prosper. But, when the people of a land, region or nation are not in sync with God's blueprint for living the land revolts against them.

The Behemoth

On March 22nd, 2023, I had a perplexing dream where I was in the back of my home looking down at Kaneohe Bay at what looked like a very old barge. The barge was swaying back and forth in the ocean's current, but as I looked closer, I realized that it wasn't a barge-it was Noah's Ark. Then out of nowhere emerged a large hippopotamus from beneath the surface of the water (the deep) and attacked the Ark biting it as hard as it could. When I woke from this dream it was obvious to me that Noah's ark represented God's desire to reach the Lost in Hawaii, but I wasn't sure what the hippo symbolized.

Job 40:15-24 describes the hippo or behemoth in the natural:

Behold, Behemoth (the hippo), which I made as I made you; he eats grass like an ox. Behold, his strength in his loins, and his power in the muscles of his belly. He makes his tail stiff like a cedar; the sinews of his thighs are knit together. His bones are tubes of bronze, his limbs like bars of iron. "He is the first of the works of God; let him who made him bring near his sword! For the mountains yield food for him where all the wild beasts play. Under the lotus plants he lies, in the shelter of the reeds and in the marsh. For his shade the lotus trees cover him; the willows of the brook surround him. Behold, if the river is turbulent he is not frightened; he is confident though Jordan rushes against his mouth. Can one take him by his eyes, or pierce his nose with a snare?

As I pondered the meaning of this dream it became obvious to me that the hippo was a spiritual being or demonic assignment that had been sent to oppose the coming move of God. But I still did not understand why the hippo had the legal right to bite the ark.

Six months later on September 5, 2023, I had second dream about a hippopotamus. In this dream I was looking down from a high place above Murakami stadium in Honolulu where the University of Hawaii baseball team plays its' games. *Mura* means superior village and *Kami* means 'god' or 'above' (Wikipedia, Murakami Surname).

As I looked down, I was shocked to see a large hippopotamus emerging from a large swath of garbage in the middle of the field as a vortex opened up and the hippo's hiding place was revealed. In response I wanted to tell those who were in charge of the stadium, "Hey, there's a hippo living underneath your baseball field" as they were totally unaware of the hippo's presence and the garbage it was living in.

Through my conversations with Paul Cox, I have come to understand that the hippo or behemoth is a demonic system tied to sexual immorality. In November 2023 Paul Cox and I facilitated the second annual apostolic integrated healing conference in Hawaii. On the third and final day of the conference I felt, by physical discernment, a gripping sensation in the area of my groin and knew immediately that the Lord wanted to deal with sexual immorality in Hawaii. The thought then came to me, "Is this the Behemoth?" I posed the question to Paul, and he confirmed, via discernment, that the Lord wanted to deal with the Behemoth or beast system. The conference attenders, including Paul and I, repented and renounced the sexual sins of Hawaii including abortion, adultery, bestiality, homosexuality and incest.

Shortly after Paul discerned that an apostolic gate had manifested in our midst. As people walked through this spiritual gate people laughed, cried, shook, trembled, kneeled, fell and jumped for joy. We were undone, wrecked and overwhelmed by the manifest presence of the Lord.

What is an Apostolic Gate?

A gate is obviously an entrance to someplace. A spiritual gate is an opening into a heavenly place or dimension (Genesis 28:17). So what is an apostolic gate? An apostolic gate is a heavenly dimension filled with signs, wonders and miracles (2 Corinthians 12:12). It is a heavenly portal that ushers you into the King's supernatural domain (1 Corinthians 4:20). Those who operate in this domain are filled with power to pull down the strongholds of the enemy so the Body of Christ may release the kingdom of God (healing and deliverance) as directed by the Holy Spirit. The apostle Paul operated in this realm as his ministry was hallmarked by powerful signs and wonders that followed him whenever he preached the gospel of the kingdom drawing the Gentiles to Jesus.

> *For I will not venture to speak of anything except what Christ has accomplished through me to bring the Gentiles to obedience—by word and deed, by the power of signs and wonders, by the power of the Spirit of God—so that from Jerusalem and all the way around to Illyricum I have fulfilled the ministry of the gospel of Christ; and thus I make it my ambition to preach the gospel, not where Christ has already been named, lest I build on someone else's foundation, but as it is written, "Those who have never been told of him will see, and those who have never heard will understand." Romans 15:18-21 (ESV)*

Earthquake Evangelism:

After the Integrated Apostolic Conference concluded a woman named Leah left to return home. As she drove away her cousin, who is incarcerated in a major penitentiary behind our church facility called her and blurted, "Did you feel the earthquake?" She said, "I did not." He went on to explain that 17 men in his cell block, all of Hawaiian ancestry, had just felt an earthquake shake the prison. In response, Leah shared how the power of God had just fallen at the conference's conclusion. Her cousin, not a believer, was blown away. Recognizing that he was open to Jesus, she led him to the Lord!

Think about the possibilities of what the Lord would do if the church dedicated itself to be a pure and spotless bride unhindered by the weight of sexual sin and abortion. I truly believe we'd see more divinely orchestrated encounters similar to what Paul and Silas experienced when the Philippian jailer yelled, "Sirs, what must I do to be saved?"

Only the Sons of God Can Break the Curse Off the Earth!
Romans 8:19-21 (TPT) cries out:

> *The entire universe is standing on tiptoe, yearning to see the unveiling of God's glorious sons and daughters! For against its will the universe (the earth or creation) itself has had to endure the empty futility resulting from the consequences of human sin. But now, with eager expectation all creation longs for freedom from its slavery to decay and to experience with us the wonderful freedom coming to God's children.*

What does it mean to be the sons (and daughters of God) and what role do we have in transforming the land where we live?

- Matthew 5:9 says that we are peacemakers. I believe the word peacemaker has two meanings: 1) The word shalom or peace means, 'complete' or 'whole'. The sons of God are peacemakers because they are able, through the ministry of the Holy Spirit, to retrieve the pieces of people's broken hearts and make them whole and 2) When we lead others to Jesus, we effect peace between them and God. The broken world in which we live is in desperate need of peacemakers.

- Matthew 16:15 says that we are able set captives free meaning that we have been empowered by God to set people free from debilitating bondages such as anger, bitterness, hatred, infirmity and rejection to name just a few. We have been empowered by God's Spirit to pull down the strongholds that keep people in misery.

- Matthew 5:43-48 says that because we have experienced God's unconditional love for us we are able to love our enemies unconditionally even when they persecute us. I believe this means that we have been called by God to model what *agape* love looks like to those around us.

- Romans 8:14 says that we are led by the Spirit of God. If we are diligent to follow what God is leading us to do (see John 5:19), He will give us supernatural solutions for the societal challenges people are facing across the globe and in the land where we live.

- Matthew 5:6 says that the sons of God hunger and thirst after righteousness. This means that out of our passion for God and our desire to align ourselves with His blueprint for living, we will perpetually dispense both His presence and blessings.

All of creation (the land) is eagerly waiting for the *huios* (sons and daughters of God) to be revealed because only the *huios* are able to heal the land. Let me repeat this one more time. Only the sons of God can heal the land!

Prayer to Reconcile, Reunite and Restore Me to the Land Where I Live

Lord, I come on behalf of myself and the sins of my entire generational line back to before the beginning of time. I renounce and repent for all of us who engaged in ungodly sexual activities outside the will of God on the specific land areas where we lived. We have repeatedly broken your covenantal laws, clearly laid out in Exodus 20:14 and Leviticus 18:1-30, which instruct us not to:

- Commit adultery
- Have sex with an animal.
- Have sex with any family member.
- Have sex with someone of the same gender.
- Abort our children (which is patterned after the burning of our children in the fires of Molech).

Lord, please forgive us for defiling the land areas where we have lived through infidelity, and through the murder of the next generation. I recognize that because we have been unfaithful to You, the land You betrothed to us has issued a divorce decree to us, and I repent for our unwillingness to follow Your Word. From this day forward, I pledge my personal fidelity to You and the land where I live.

Lord, please:

- Cleanse us of all defilement and guilt resulting from our unholy sexual activities and the murder of the innocent.

- Sever every ungodly soul tie between me and the land areas where we have sinned sexually.

- By Your grace and mercy, please burn up the divorce papers that the land served us, and cleanse by your blood every geographic area where we have lived.

Lord, as the Lion of Judah, please release the sound and frequency of Your mighty roar and set free all generational spirit and soul parts that have been entrapped in the land; remove all parts from the ungodly length, depth, width and height. I also ask You, Lord Jesus, to wield Your sword as the Son of Man and sever me and my generational line from the grip of the Rephaim, which show themselves as the dead ones, departed spirits or shades (Proverbs 2:16-18, 9:13-18; Isaiah 26:14).

Lord, please complete the process of reconciling, reuniting and restoring me to the land You have given us by destroying every ungodly generational library to which the enemy has access. This has resulted in us being spit out and/or has caused the lands where we live or have lived to come against us. Lord, I am truly sorry that we have wounded Your heart and have given the enemy the legal right to wreak havoc upon our families and the lands where we live.

Lord, please release the authority that is available to me through Jesus Christ, so that I may advance

Your kingdom in the land you have given me. Lord, for me, my family line, and my descendants, please establish our connections to the land that are in accordance with Your original design. Amen

8. A Lack of Love and Compassion for the Sick

And if I have prophetic powers, and understand all mysteries and all knowledge, and if I have all faith, so as to remove mountains, but have not love, I am nothing. If I speak in the tongues of men and of angels, but have not love, I am a noisy gong or a clanging cymbal. If I give away all I have, and if I deliver up my body to be burned, but have not love, I gain nothing. Love is patient and kind; love does not envy or boast; it is not arrogant or rude. It does not insist on its own way; it is not irritable or resentful; it does not rejoice at wrongdoing, but rejoices with the truth. Love bears all things, believes all things, hopes all things, endures all things. 1 Corinthians 13:1-7 (ESV)

An Amazing Miracle:
In the late 1990's I listened to a message left on my phone by a pastor inviting me to his home where a close friend of his and his wife were to share and minister. When I showed up at his front door he said, "Hi Rob, what are you doing here?" Surprised by his response I reminded him that he had left a message inviting me to his home on my phone. He thought for a moment and said, "I must have dialed the wrong number. It doesn't matter come inside."

As the evening unfolded his friend told a story I will never forget. After arriving in a third world nation to minister she was driven to a village. While walking through the village with her guide/interpreter she saw a woman caked from head to toe in mud. As she looked at the woman the Holy Spirit whispered to her, "Jan, go over to her and love on her for me by giving her a hug." Normally this godly woman would have obeyed the Lord but because she was wearing a newly purchased white pants suit, she replied, "But Lord, I just purchased this new pants suit, and I don't want it to get dirty." Then Lord spoke gently a second time, "Go over to her and give her a hug." The internal struggle continued, and the woman objected, "But Lord, she's caked with mud!" The Lord firmly said, "Give her a hug!"

Wanting to obey the Lord, Jan asked the interpreter to ask the mud caked woman if she could hug her. The woman agreed and Jan gave her a big hug. Suddenly the woman began to jump up and down like a pogo stick screaming with joy. Jan asked the interpreter to ask the woman what had happened and after asking the woman replied, "She said, 'I was blind, but now I can see!'"

Sometimes people don't get healed because we have not ministered to them in the spirit of compassion-the love of Christ. What's the lesson here? It is the love of God that heals. It's not our anointing, it's His anointing and that anointing is His lovingkindness that endures forever.

9. Self-sufficiency

Unless the Lord builds the house, those who build it labor in vain. Unless the Lord watches over the city, the watchman stays awake in vain. Psalm 127:1 (ESV)

It is the Spirit who gives life; the flesh profits nothing. The words that I speak to you are spirit, and are life. John 6:63 (NKJV)

My Dysfunctional, Performance Driven Family:
I grew up in a family of achievers, or at least I perceived that I did. My father, Bert, went to Dartmouth in Hanover, New Hampshire and my mother to Yale in New Haven, Connecticut. My cousins were also Ivy Leaguers, so I grew up feeling like I had to prove myself academically by upholding the family standard of excellence.

This standard was further downloaded into my soul when my grandfather held a writing contest for me and my six cousins. It was a ten-page essay about something that I can't recall to this day. But I do remember that the top four finishers would receive $25 to $100 dollars.

On the day of judgment, we met with our grandfather to hear him share his thoughts about our essays. I can't remember what my grandfather said, but I do remember wanting to place somewhere in at least the top four. I breathed a sigh of relief when my grandfather awarded me $25 dollars for my efforts. Unfortunately, because there were only four monetary awards three of my cousins left the room disappointed.

Suffice to say I grew up in a performance-oriented culture that promoted achievement. This led to decades of striving and self-effort that eventually led to a prolonged period of burnout and depression in my early 40's. And sadly, as a church planter my performance mindset led to years of trying to build God's church by my own strength and self-effort.

During a two-month period of depression I went to Elijah House in Post Falls, Idaho. Before my first appointment with my prayer counselor, I had a dream of going up a hill on a skateboard powering it with my right leg. In the second half of the dream, I stepped into a cable car and it lifted me up toward the top of a tall mountain.

Later, after sharing the dream with my counselor she said, "Based on the issues you listed on our ministry questionnaire, the Lord has brought you to Elijah House to take you off the mountain of performance so He can lift you up His mountain in the cable car of His grace."

Many five-fold officers (especially pastors) and leaders leave the ministry or are discouraged because their efforts have not produced the fruit of their dreams and aspirations. Hebrews 4:11 (ESV) says:

> *Let us therefore strive to enter that rest, so that no one may fall by the same sort of disobedience.*

10. **The Holy Spirit Has Been Locked Up**

> *And I tell you, you are Peter, and on this rock I will build my church, and the gates of hell shall not prevail against it. I will give you the keys of the kingdom of heaven, and whatever you bind on earth shall be bound in heaven, and whatever you loose on earth shall be loosed in heaven. Matthew 16:18-19 (ESV)*

According to Britannica.com **apostolic succession** is the teaching that Catholic bishops represent a direct, uninterrupted line of continuity from the first apostles. According to this teaching, bishops possess certain special powers passed down to them from the apostles; these consist primarily of the right to confirm church members, to ordain priests, to consecrate other bishops, and to rule over the clergy and church members in their diocese (an area made up of several congregations). Put more simply,

'Apostolic Succession' is the uninterrupted transmission of spiritual authority from the New Testament apostles through successive popes and bishops. This doctrine originated from Mathew 16:18-19 where Jesus designated Peter as the rock upon which He would build his church. Peter is thus believed to have been the first pope and thus the papacy is a continuous line of apostolic successors.

A Kairos Moment:
Why does this matter and how does it pertain to an outage of divine power in the church? On February 28, 2013, Pope Benedict XVI unexpectedly stepped down as Pope. Two weeks later, Pope Francis, Archbishop of Buenos Aires was elected as the new Pope. During the two-week interlude when Pope Benedict stepped down and Pope Francis was elected, a *Kairos* moment from the Lord presented itself to my dear friend and colleague Dr. Paul L. Cox. Paul called me and shared that the Lord had shown him that the Holy Spirit (the source of kingdom power) has been locked away by the traditions of man, such as the doctrine of Apostolic Succession in the Catholic Church.

Ask yourself this: did Jesus give the Apostle Peter the keys to the kingdom of heaven so only popes and bishops could storm the gates of hell? No! Jesus gave Peter the keys to the kingdom of heaven to 'empower' the people of God to set the captives free (through healing and deliverance). If this wasn't true, why then were Stephen (Acts 6:8) and Philipp (Acts 8:6) able to perform signs and wonders as neither of them men were apostles? On the contrary, these two men were everyday believers who possessed the keys of the kingdom heaven to take down hell and set the captives free.

In response to what we believe God was revealing to us during this *Kairos* moment we prayed:

"Lord Jesus, we decree and declare that You are giving us the opportunity now to lay claim to the keys You entrusted to Peter to access the kingdom power to build Your church. In Jesus name. Amen."

Could it be that we have been suffering from a power outage in the church because of a centuries old doctrine that has kept the people of God on the sideline and the power of God locked up in a vault? Since the keys of the kingdom of heaven have never belonged to any pope, we asked the Lord if we could take them back for the entire *ekklesia* not just the papacy.

In this chapter I have mentioned ten reasons why there is a power shortage in the church. In my humble opinion I think striving, self-effort and jumping ahead of God's timing has capped the Lord's power from flowing. Years of performance-oriented ministry led me to suffer from countless cold sores, angst and frustration. But, once I got off my skateboard and stepped into the cable car of God's grace, He flipped the power switch and the current of His *dunamis* power flowed resulting in numerous signs, wonders and miracles.

In Chapter Three, Paul Cox will continue to explain why today's church is suffering from a power outage.

CHAPTER THREE:
OUR PIPES ARE CLOGGED
PAUL L COX

Will it ever end? If it does end, what will my life look like? On May 30, 2024, it will have been four years of experiencing intense deliverance. Several times during these four years, I thought, "Now it is over." However, I was wrong; it did not end until June 12, 2024.

Pentecost 2020 was May 30th. A small group of us gathered at Aslan's Place to wait on the Lord. A prophetic friend of mine asked if she could stand in front of me. Permission granted, she pointed at me as I stood and said, "The Lord is going to clean out your DNA." I felt a shock wave hit me and fell back into my seat. Immediately, I could sense evil coming off me.

The next day I woke up and could feel a violent, moving headache indicating the flow of evil coming off. I could sense the Lord removing evil from my DNA and RNA; and could also feel ungodly thrones being removed and the windows of the heavens being realigned. It was constant and was wearing me out every day. Still doing ministry, the deliverance I felt was not the client's but my own. I was trying to live a normal life with my wife, doing the everyday stuff we have to do; but it was very, very exhausting.

As the deliverance continued, I noticed a pattern. The more spiritual toxic waste that left me, the more revelation I received. The Lord gave me revelation about the mighty ones, the deep darkness, the kings and the firmament. Every time there was more revelation, there was also more deliverance. The most profound revelation and discernment was the realm of Grace.

Now four years later, I have had a thought, "What if we have not really understood why the church does not operate in the power we see in the book of Acts?" What if the secret to a powerful Christian life is NOT more information but more power.

Pondering this, I stumbled onto a verse, John 15:3, that I had read many times:

> *You are already clean because of the word which I have spoken to you.* [1]

Now I understood.

Sometime around 1996, a friend called from Alaska and said, "Paul, I have a verse for you. It is Matthew 8:16:"

> *When evening had come, they brought to Him many who were demon-possessed. And He cast out the spirits with <u>a word</u>, and healed all who were sick...*

Do you know what that means?" I think I understood. In the next prayer session, I opened in prayer and then said, "Leave." With just that word, I somehow locked into what the Lord was doing and could feel deliverance coming off the person. I was aware of the deliverance for, sometimes, up to three days. As time went by, I would feel the deliverance only until I went to bed.

I was stunned by the revelation. Jesus had simply spoken a word and His power had cleaned out all the defilement in the disciples. It was a total deliverance! What does this mean? Now, the power of God could fully flow through them, and they would be able to walk supernaturally in signs, wonders, healings, deliverance and miracles. It was not what the disciples did that mattered. Let me repeat that – it was not what the disciples did that mattered! It was what the Father did that mattered. Once the resistance to His power was removed, they could fully do what the Father was doing.

What are the implications of this? Essentially this means that our ability to do what the Father is doing is not about what we know and how we perform, but rather it is about being so cleaned out from the defilement of our lives and generational line, so that His power can flow through us.

Contemplating what has happened to us over the centuries, I realized we literally have become clogged by generational toxic waste. An image came to my mind, and I searched the internet. I found it: Before me was a picture of a clogged pipe with its interior crusted by decades of gunk that had solidified. The water flow was restricted to a trickle.

A truth: Generational issues have so clogged us that His power cannot flow freely. We need the PLUMMER to speak the word over us and set us free.

I can already hear what many of those in the church say, "A person does not need deliverance!" But we must look at the evidence that we do need deliverance. Scripture is clear, and those who have received prayer ministry testify to the freedom they have experienced. One must literally put their heads in the sand in order to ignore this truth.

So, what is the church's answer to our dilemma of being clogged? Please notice the sarcasm!

- Meet weekly with a person to discuss how I feel about being clogged

- Attend a seminar on why all pipes stopped being clogged by 100AD
- Declare at worship services that I am not clogged and I am victorious
- Realize that by admitting I am clogged I will gain freedom from cloggness
- Cover up the smell of the cloggness by using essential oils
- Use natural remedies and supplements on the pipe to remedy the cloggness
- Get rid of all sugar and flour to solve the problem of the clog
- Purchase magnets to correct the clog
- Declare daily, "I am not clogged."
- Go into a meditative state so you can overcome cloggness
- Every Sunday, go to church to be told you are not really clogged

Ignoring our condition is only the first part of the problem.

---

[1] John 15:3

Chapter Four:
IGNORING THE POWER
Paul L Cox

There is a secondary problem - a tremendous resistance to allowing the power of God to operate in the church or in believers. Did I really just write that? It is not only true today but is also historically true. The children of Israel, even though they had benefited from His power and were rescued from slavery, refused to go near Mount Sinai because of the display of His power.

I have my own reluctant journey in His power. Growing up as a Southern Baptist and American Baptist I had no idea about the power of God. Of course, we read about His power but that was in the Bible and certainly did not happen today. Nothing changed when I became a Baptist youth pastor and later a church pastor. It was not until 1988, that the Lord began my walk in His power. I was in my eighth year of pastoring and was rather frustrated with the lack of progress of the church. Church was wonderful, but the growth that I had anticipated had not happened and I felt stagnant. One morning I was at home, enjoying the sun coming through the sliding glass doors and reading in the book of Proverbs. As I read Proverbs 23:18, *There is surely a future hope for you, and your hope will not be cut off*, I felt a strong physical sensation on my head that swept downward over my entire body. What was that?!? I had no language for what had just happened. Over the next few days, I asked many of my friends if they could explain it, but no answers came.

After leading my first deliverance, a therapist asked me to

pray for someone who had Multiple Personality Disorder (now known as dissociative identity disorder). One Sunday afternoon, five of us gathered together with the client. As we prayed with her, a three-year-old alter came forward and talked with us. Suddenly she said, "Paul, do you want to see her totally healed?" I realized the Lord was talking to me and I felt a 'whoosh' as well as power on my head. God's power filled the room. The next day we entered that same room and felt a presence we could not explain. Then, walking into the sanctuary we could feel the same presence flowing across the front of the sanctuary.

In the Fall of 1991, after leaving the church and starting an interim pastorate in the San Diego area, I was visiting another American Baptist pastor at his home. I was talking on the phone when I felt a strong presence on my head, which continued to grow stronger and stronger. Ending the call, I walked a few feet and was literally thrown on the floor by more power than I had ever felt. Waves of power came over me for more than an hour. I'd experienced an encounter with the Living God, which would forever change my life.

Later, around 1994, a young man came to our youth group. As the group dispersed, we started talking and he shared with me that he was a fifth-generation Mormon as well as a practicing Buddhist who often practiced astral projection. I asked him to tell me about Mormonism. The friendly conversation turned into an argument, and I was not making any progress in proving my point. Then I had an idea. I asked if I could try something; he agreed. I said, "Anger, come forth." His eyes rolled back in his head as he made a hissing sound. I was no longer talking to him but to an evil entity, so I called him by name and told him to come to the front. "What was that," he asked. I replied, "That's who's controlling you;" to which he responded, "What do I do?" My answer, "Accept Jesus as your personal Savior." He did, and I felt the Holy Spirit come into him with a 'whoosh', like filing a bag. He had encountered the manifested power of God.

Over the following years, I have experienced many times when waves of the power of God have flooded over me. Often, I am unable to stand and fall to the floor. His Power is real and life changing.

I did not know that the Lord was now interested in displaying His power to others. But then, while still pastoring, I was invited to speak at an American Baptist Church in the San Diego area. After sharing about Moses seeking the Lord's glory and the reality of His glory tied to the cherubim in Ezekiel chapters one and ten, I asked the Lord to show His glory. His power fell on the people and these American Baptists were on the floor under His power. The reaction was not what I had hoped. The entire worship team left the church and there were intense negative discussions about what had happened. I had entered a new dimension of my life, as the Lord would lead me to speak at other places where He would display His glory. Sadly, it never seemed to have a favorable response.

I was invited to speak at another church that we were attending. I was aware of an increase of power on me during the afternoon, so I called the pastor and said, "Donna and I have to talk to you because I just want to warn you something might happen tonight." He responded that he'd seen just about everything, so we went to the church. They were singing a worship song with the lyrics, "Lord, do with me whatever You want to do." I thought, "Oh, don't sing that; please do not sing that song." The pastor then told me to just give my sermon and then he'd dismiss anyone who wanted to go, after which I could 'do my thing'. We did that, and by the time it was over, his eyes were expressing without words, "I've never seen that before!" He never made eye contact with me again, so we left that church.

I spoke to another church in the area, and there was so much power that I was literally hanging onto the pulpit. His power fell but afterward nothing else seemed to happen at the church. Again, His power had not only been rejected but also ignored.

My friend, Rich Marshall, has a television show *God at Work* on God TV, and I was in Florida where we were taping two shows for his program. While there, I met the pastor of a four-thousand-member church in a large city. He asked me to pray for him; and as I did, we both ended up doing a little spin about ten times, and he went down on the ground. He then said, "I'm going to invite you to come to my church." I thought, "That's not going to happen," but he did invite both Rich and I to come. I was to speak on Saturday to the business leaders in the church. Sixty to seventy people attended, and we had a wonderful time. On Sunday morning, Rich was speaking in two services. The worship was so amazing that Donna and I wanted to go back to the second service and experience it again. As we sat in the front row, I discerned the arrival of the angel over the city. I walked up to Rich, who was sitting in the front waiting to speak and told him, "I think the angel of the city is here and has a tongue and a message." He answered, "What are you going to do about that?" I reply, "I'm not going to do anything, because this is not my church nor my responsibility today. I'm just coming to let you know so you can decide if you want to do something about it." I sat down.

After the pastor introduced Rich, he walked up to the pastor and whispered in his ear. The pastor said, "Paul, would you like to tell the people what is happening right now?" The sanctuary was filled with 1,500 people and I was thinking, "No, I do not want to say anything." But I went up onto the platform and said, "I believe the angel of your city is here and there is a tongue and a message." The pastor did the unthinkable and said, "Let's get the message." Sitting down, I was thinking, "Oh no, please." As one lady got up and began speaking, I said to Donna, "Nope, that's not the message." She finally finished, another lady stood and spoke strongly in a tongue, followed by the interpretation. The power of God fell on that room; and Rich, the pastor, and I were rolling around on the floor.

All around I heard screaming, and people were falling out into the aisles. The worship team began singing and I heard the pastor say, "Paul, why don't you come back." I had a difficult time standing but managed drag myself up to the front, laid my hands on several people, and His power overwhelmed all of us. People were still screaming, and deliverance was taking place. Then the pastor said, "Everyone that wants to be saved come forward." No sermon had been given, but over twelve people responded to receive the Lord. Church was dismissed, but sometime later I found out that there had been an intense discussion in the staff meeting about what I had done. Hmmm, I thought it was not what I did, but what the Lord did. Some staff people actually left the church because of what happened.

His power also came to a church in Hawaii. I was to speak one night, and I remember standing at the door thinking, "I don't know what I'm going to do." There were about 300 people present, and someone from the front row said, "I see a golden laver," and I realized a spiritual version of the tabernacle was there. I hadn't taught about the tabernacle for years, so I opened the discussion, and we had a joint Bible study about the tabernacle. I had the thought that we were to walk through the it and discern the various furnishings, though I had never done this before. I stationed the pastor and his wife at the Holy of Holies. As the people walked into the spiritual tabernacle at its gate, into the brazen altar and then the other furniture, power surges flashed through the tabernacle. People began falling as others stumbled, trying to complete the walking course. The next day, I found out that four young single men had come to service that night and had walked through the tabernacle. One of them said, "I don't know what happened in there, but demons left me." The next day, all four became Christians and then were baptized. The following Sunday, several leaders left the church, along with many of the members. It was not all good news, as many complained about what had happened and others left the church. Again, the power was rejected. Did it even matter that four young men were saved? Sorry – the whole thing didn't fit some people's theology.

In January 2021, my son, Brian, and I were invited to the San Francisco Bay area by my first intern at Aslan's Place, who is a home-school principal. We were to pray for, teach, and train a group of home-schooled elementary students. Concerned because I had been discerning the Father's power for two days, I called my friend before we went and said, "I want to warn you; something may happen, and if you don't want us to come, we won't, because I am done with churches where people don't want the power. Don't blame me later if you still want us there." He replied that he did want us, so we got ready to leave, and on the morning that we were to drive to Northern CA, I could still feel the

Father's power. I called my friend again to double check and said, "I got these words, 'Get ready, get ready, get ready.' Do you still want me to come? Because if you don't, I'm fine." He reaffirmed we should come so off we went, eventually arriving at an old elementary school. The plan was that we would meet first with the board and a couple of teachers; and later that Thursday evening with the parents and some of the kids; then, on Friday we'd be with the kids all day.

As we sat there on Thursday, I received a phrase and asked the question, "Are you ready to become the landing strip for the power of God? Because if you do not want this, I don't care; I have nothing to prove here, and this is not my school." We continued and everyone was talking when Brian said, "You have not answered my dad's question." It became very quiet as they soberly considered, and then they all said yes.

That evening, I gave a short talk to about fifty adults and kids, and then said, "I believe there is a gate of power here because I feel the Father's power; and I believe that something is going to happen tonight. If you as teachers and parents are not going to steward the power with these kids, then we will not continue because it would be a big mistake." I was very serious, but they agreed to proceed.

I felt a gate and a ten-year-old boy got up when I asked if he could feel the gate. He touched it and, bam, he was down on the floor in an open vision. I thought, "This might work!" We finally were able to help him stand, and he walked through the gate, all-the-while screaming and carrying on under the power of God. Everyone else started walking through as well, and they were also screaming as they encountered His power.

Eventually, I turned to my son and said, "I think this is

getting out of control. What are we going to do here? They are all going off the rail - parents, teachers and kids." I finally got everyone up and holding hands; and said, "We are going to need to learn to walk in the power."

The next day, we did some teachings on discernment from 9AM to noon. I discerned angels coming and giving the children different items. We had a wonderful time listening to the children share what the angels had given them. Towards lunchtime the kids were getting really squirrely, becoming more and more restless. One child asked, "When are we going to walk thru the portal?" I hadn't said anything about a portal but responded that we would wait to see what the Lord would do.

When we came back, I discerned the Holy Spirit as Wisdom and realized that there was a gate of Wisdom. First, we talked about the Holy Spirit and about Wisdom; then the first kid walked through and hit the ground again. Everyone walked through the gate and suddenly all these squirrely kids were lying on the floor and the only thing we heard for the next 30 minutes was, "Aaahhh, aaahhh." I realized that I had never seen such supernatural power in my life. Imagine a group of elementary school children without any human touch quietly resting under the power of God in His presence and experiencing open visions. Watching in amazement at those kids lying there on the floor under God's power for over a half hour, I thought, "Finally, a group that is willing to experience and walk in God's power."

Years earlier in the early 2000s, I had been in Zurich, Switzerland where we had a conference. The Pastor came up to me and said, "Paul, there's talk in the town, and they do not want you here." A sense of holy indignation rose up in me, and I became so angry in the Lord that I wrote a Declaration:

> I do not come to you with excellency of speech or with man's wisdom to declare to you the testimony of God. For I'm determined not to know anything among you but Jesus Christ and Him crucified. I come in weakness and fear, and in much trembling. My speech and my preaching are not with persuasive words, but in demonstration of the Spirit and power so that your faith will not be in the wisdom of men, but in the power of God.

> I am determined to know Jesus Christ and the power of His resurrection, and the fellowship of sharing in His sufferings, becoming like Him in His death.

> I declare that the Kingdom of God is not a matter of talk, but of power.

> I declare that we have this treasure of power in jars of clay to show this all-surpassing power is from God, and not from us.

> I declare my goal is that the God of our Lord Jesus Christ, the Father Glory, may give to you the spirit of wisdom and the revelation of the knowledge of Him, and that the eyes of your understanding may be enlightened that you may know what is the hope of His calling, what are the riches of the glory of His inheritance in the saints, and what is the exceeding greatness of His power to us who believe, according to the working of His mighty power, which He worked in Christ when He raised Him from the dead and seated Him at His right hand in the

heavenly places.

According to the Word of God, I stand against all who have a form of godliness but deny its power.

I stand in the name of the Lord Jesus against every and all religious spirits that seek to confuse, disrupt or misinterpret what I say.

I declare that only the Lord God can create spiritual gifts. The enemy can only distort, twist, and pervert what God has already created.

I declare that it is time for the Church to take back all spiritual gifts stolen by the enemy, and allow the Holy Spirit to use them for the sake of the advancement of the Kingdom of God.

I declare that everything I do during our time together is in submission to the Lord Jesus Christ and the leadership of this conference (or church), and that I do everything in the name of the Lord Jesus Christ whose blood was shed on the cross for us, and who rose from the dead and is seated at the right hand of the Father.

I declare that His is the kingdom, and the power, and the glory forever. Amen

Are you willing to unplug from the world and yield to His power?

CHAPTER FIVE:

GRACE AS POWER

PAUL L COX

As a child I learned Ephesians 2:8-9:

> *For by grace you have been saved through faith, and that not of yourselves; it is the gift of God, not of works, lest anyone should boast. (NKJV)*

Vine's Complete Expository Dictionary renders the Greek definition of Grace as

> *charis* has various uses, (a) objective, that which bestows or occasions pleasure, delight, or causes favorable regard; it is applied, e.g., to beauty, or gracefulness of person, Luke 2:40; act, 2 Cor. 8:6, or speech, Luke 4:22, RV, "words of grace" (KJV, "gracious words"); Col. 4:6; (b) subjective, (1) on the part of the bestower, the friendly disposition from which the kindly act proceeds, graciousness, loving-kindness, goodwill generally, e.g., Acts 7:10; especially with reference to the divine favor or "grace," e.g., Acts 14:26 [1]

We have correctly seen grace as the wonderful favor of the Lord towards us, which leads us to salvation. But the concept is so much more!

As a pastor, in studying the word 'grace', I was shocked to discover that in the Greek it is actually a power word historically.[2] Let's look at both the Old and New Testament.

Old Testament

On a Tuesday, while praying for a person who had come for ministry, I felt something very strongly and said, "I don't know what this is, and I don't think I am supposed to do anything right now." The client then started vibrating under the power of God, was healed of some recurring issues and set free miraculously by the manifestation of power.

I called a prophetic friend and told her, "Something has happened to me." She replied, "I see golden pipes on the back of your head." I had no idea what she was talking about.

I did a search and found the golden pipes mentioned in Zachariah 4:1-7, 11-14 (ESV):

> *And the angel who talked with me came again and woke me, like a man who is awakened out of his sleep. And he said to me, "What do you see?" I said, "I see, and behold, a lampstand all of gold, with a bowl on the top of it, and seven lamps on it, with seven lips on each of the lamps that are on the top of it. And there are two olive trees by it, one on the right of the bowl and the other on its left." And I said to the angel who talked with me, "What are these, my lord?" Then the angel who talked with me answered and said to me, "Do you not know what these are?" I said, "No, my lord." Then he said to me, "This is the word of the Lord to Zerubbabel: Not by might, nor by power, but by my Spirit, says the Lord of hosts. Who are you, O great mountain? Before Zerubbabel you shall become a plain. And he shall bring forward the top stone amid shouts of 'Grace, grace to it!'"*

Then I said to him, "What are these two olive trees on the right and the left of the lampstand?" And a second time I answered and said to him, "What are these two branches of the olive trees, which are beside the two golden pipes from which the golden oil is poured out?" He said to me, "Do you not know what these are?" I said, "No, my lord." Then he said, "These are the two anointed ones who stand by the Lord of the whole earth."

This is exactly what I was feeling on the back of my head — two golden pipes that seemed to boil with the oil. The power on the back on my neck and back was burning hot. Note that in the context of the pipes the Lord is speaking of Grace and power. It is not by our power but by His Spirit. There is then a shout of Grace, Grace.

New Testament

As I explored the New Testament for verses on grace the connection with power became evident.

Ephesians 3:6-7 (NKJV): *... that the Gentiles should be fellow heirs, of the same body, and partakers of His promise in Christ through the gospel, of which I became a minister according to the gift of the <u>grace</u> of God given to me by the effective working of His <u>power</u>.*

2 Corinthians 12:9 (ESV): *And He said to me, "My <u>grace</u> is sufficient for you, for My strength is made perfect in weakness." Therefore, most gladly I will rather boast in my infirmities, that the <u>power</u> of Christ may rest upon me.*

Acts 4:33 (NKJV): *And with great <u>power</u> the apostles gave witness to the resurrection of the Lord Jesus. And great <u>grace</u> was upon them all.*

Acts 6:8 (ESV); *And Stephen, full of <u>grace and power</u>, did great wonders and signs among the people.*

Acts 18:27–28 (ESV): *And when he [Paul] wished to cross to Achaia, the brothers encouraged him and wrote to the disciples to welcome him. When he arrived, he greatly helped those who through <u>grace</u> had believed, for <u>powerfully</u> refuted the Jews in public, showing by the Scriptures that the Christ was Jesus."*

2 Corinthians 12:8–9 (NKJV): *Concerning this thing I pleaded with the Lord three times that it might depart from me. And He said to me, "<u>My grace</u> is sufficient for you, for My strength is made perfect in weakness." Therefore most gladly I will rather boast in my infirmities, that the <u>power</u> of Christ may rest upon me.*

Have you pondered why Paul was able to evangelize so powerfully in the midst of pagan Rome? I have. What happened in Paul's world to so dramatically affect society that thousands came into the Kingdom of God; the final result of which was the overthrow of an empire? I had no answer until my wife, Donna, and I took a dream cruise on the Mediterranean Sea for our forty-fifth wedding university.

We flew to Rome, Italy and traveled to the port of Rome to board our ten-day cruise of the Mediterranean. Returning to the port, we boarded a bus tour of Rome that stopped at the cathedral of St Paul, the one stop of the day. Clearly, it was a very important stop as we all made a bee line to the bathrooms. Since docking, I had been very aware of intense evil on the land, continually asking the Lord to remove the oppression, but there was no relief! As we walked to the bathroom, which was on the right side of the cathedral, I hit a wall of power and, 'woosh', all the evil was gone! I wondered, "What is this power doing here? Isn't this a Roman Catholic church?" I told Donna to check it out, asking her the same question. She returned to the bus, and I decided to venture into the cathedral. Walking along, I moved into that power again, still wondering what in the world was happening. My eyes moved upward to a sign just to the left of where I was standing, "The burial place of the Apostle Paul;" and I thought, "He is really buried here, and the anointing remains." Instantly I understood something. Paul wrote in 1 Corinthians 2:1-5 (ESV):

> *And I, when I came to you, brothers, did not come proclaiming to you the testimony of God with lofty speech or wisdom. For I decided to know nothing among you except Jesus Christ and him crucified. And I was with you in weakness and in fear and much trembling, and my speech and my message were not in plausible words of wisdom, but in demonstration of the Spirit and of power, so that your faith might not rest in the wisdom of men but in the power of God.*

Here was the answer. Paul walked in such power that as he traveled into cities, the power of God resting on him delivered both cities and people whose minds had been blinded to the Gospel; and they clearly understood the truth about Jesus Christ and surrendered their lives to Him. The power of Grace led to their redemption.

What is the secret to the *Power Outage*? Simple! Yield to the Lord and declare to Him, "I will no longer restrict Your power from flowing in my life." Please turn the Power back on.

In Chapter Four, Rob will break down the difference between equipping the church and training the Body for works of ministry

---

[1] Vine, W. E., Unger, M. F., & White, W., Jr. (1996). In *Vine's Complete Expository Dictionary of Old and New Testament Words* (Vol. 2, p. 277). T. Nelson.

[2] Conzelmann, H., & Zimmerli, W. (1964). In G. Kittel, G. W. Bromiley, & G. Friedrich (eds.), *Theological Dictionary of the New Testament* (electronic ed., vol. 9, p. 395). Eerdmans. Conzelmann, H, & Zimmerli, W. (1964)1964

CHAPTER SIX:

EQUIPPING THE CHURCH FOR MAXIMUM IMPACT

ROB GROSS

Pioneering:

In 1996, I had a dream about pioneering. In the dream I was sitting on a schooner or western cowboy-type wagon, leading other pioneers also on wagons to an unknown place. Pulled by a train of horses, I could feel the wind at my face; but suddenly spears and arrows whooshed by my head nearly missing me. Out of instinct I looked ahead for some place to escape from the attack behind and saw a circular shaped forest with an opening up ahead. I headed toward the opening, along with the other pioneers, and drove through the entrance. Once inside the forest I immediately noticed a small lake that was on fire and a small log cabin behind it.

When I woke up from the dream, I knew in my spirit that God was calling me to pioneer something new, but I had no idea what that something meant. In the years that followed I received multiple words from both apostles and prophets that confirmed the dream.

To illustrate the position a pioneer, or innovator, finds himself in, we can view the Innovation-Adoption Curve:[1]

Radical change in any facet of society, including the church, is preceded by a group of individuals who are willing to go where no man or woman has gone before, the First Century apostles among them. They overturned the religious system of their day, which was keeping people in spiritual bondage to sin; and released the power of the Holy Spirit that has radically transformed religious people into God's sons and daughters down through generations to the present day.

Is this all there is Lord?

As a pastor, a normal week goes something like this:

- Saturday and Monday: I'm off
- Tuesday: I start praying about the Sunday message, and sometimes start typing it out on my iPad
- Wednesday: I prepare for and lead my staff meeting
- Thursday and Friday: I meet people in the church to 'father' and or counsel
- Sunday: I preach.

After doing this for years, I realized I was managing instead of leading the church and I began to ask the Lord, "Is this all there is to ministry?" My heart longed to see and

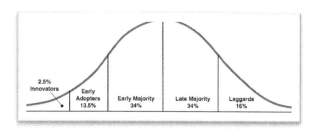

experience what I read about in the Book of Acts; to see God's people activated to 'do the stuff'. You know, the kingdom stuff where miracles were normative, people bound by demonic bondages were transformed for the better, and non-believers wholeheartedly gave their lives to Jesus.

An Airplane Shaped Training Center:
In 1998 I had a dream where I was in an airplane-shaped training center that was preparing and sending believers into the harvest fields of the world. Little did I know at that time that 25 years later I would co-launch the Kingdom Institute with Paul Cox.

Did the First Century Church focus on training God's people?
The Bible reveals three passages about training in the New Testament:

> *Now those who were scattered because of the persecution that arose over Stephen traveled as far as Phoenicia and Cyprus and Antioch, speaking the word to no one except Jews. But there were some of them, men of Cyprus and Cyrene, who on coming to Antioch spoke to the Hellenists also, preaching the Lord Jesus. And the hand of the Lord was with them, and a great number who believed turned to the Lord. The report of this came to the ears of the church in Jerusalem, and they sent Barnabas to Antioch. When he came and saw the grace of God, he was glad, and he exhorted them all to remain faithful to the Lord with steadfast purpose, for he was a good man, full of the Holy Spirit and of faith. And a great many people were added to the Lord. So Barnabas went to Tarsus to look for Saul, and when he had found him, he brought him to Antioch.*

For a whole year they met with the church and taught a great many people. And in Antioch the disciples were first called Christians. Acts 11:19-26 (ESV)

And he entered the synagogue and for three months spoke boldly, reasoning and persuading them about the kingdom of God. But when some became stubborn and continued in unbelief, speaking evil of the Way before the congregation, he withdrew from them and took the disciples with him, reasoning daily in the hall of Tyrannus. This continued for two years, so that all the residents of Asia heard the word of the Lord, both Jews and Greeks. Acts 19:8-10 (ESV)

But solid food is for the mature, for those who have their powers of discernment trained by constant practice to distinguish good from evil. Hebrews 5:14 (ESV)

David VS Goliath (DVGJiu-Jitsu Center):

My son, Brandon, co-owns and operates a Jiu-Jitsu Gym. The gym, at this time, has 400 members and is a faith-based entity that trains men, women and children. As I have chatted with my son about Jiu-Jitsu over the years, he has repeatedly shared with me that Jiu-Jitsu is more than a sport, it's a lifestyle. The gym where members train rigorously, which is located upstairs in our church facility is open six days a week. Whether white belt beginners or black belt experts, everyone is committed to learning the basics and strategies involved with the sport.

As with the gym protocol, I submit to you that if we truly want to make kingdom impact in our society today, we need to think strategically about training God's people to heal the sick, deliver the demonized at multiple levels. As our nation and society continues to spiral out of control, more and more people are dealing with trauma, depression, gender confusion, STD's and more. If the church continues to meet only to worship and hear a weekend message, then we will not be the healing/delivering salt and light that Jesus wants us to be.

A Mid-Twenties Male Gets Healed of an STD:
Over 20 years ago, a young man gave his life to Jesus after hearing the Gospel message from one of the women in our church. While having breakfast together at a restaurant this young man asked if we could meet at a more private place. We went back to my office, and he shared that he had just been diagnosed with an incurable sexually transmitted disease. Because he wanted to become a missionary he was bummed out, as you might imagine.

During our breakfast, I had a painful sensation in my groin alerting me to the possibility that he was dealing with a sexual issue of some kind. So, when he shared his problem, I was not surprised. Little did I realize that the Holy Spirit was about to perform an extraordinary miracle for this young man. In fact, I had little faith that God would heal him when I offered to pray for him. After he acknowledged that he wanted prayer, I prayed a faithless prayer asking God to heal him. To my utter shock, after I mumbled a prayer over him he declared by faith, "I'm healed!" He then got up and said, "I'm going back to my doctor to get re-tested!"

Two weeks later, the young man called me on the phone and shared that he was healed. He went on to share that his doctor told him that he didn't need to get retested. Contrary to the doctor's opinion, he insisted on a re-test; and the rest is history.

Sometimes we are oblivious to the fact that people, whether young, old or somewhere in-between, are in dire need of God's healing touch. Yet, if the church does not provide ongoing, regular training for God's people, they will not be prepared to pray for them when the Holy Spirit gives them the opportunity.

What is God up to?

He's aligning us with His governmental order. God's government has five legs (imagine a five-legged stool). Why is the Lord doing this? Three reasons: First, the Lord is aligning His government is because it is not yet aligned with the Word of God.

In this present season the offices of pastor and teacher are prominent. Lord, we are grateful for Your pastors and teachers, but we acknowledge that no structure can excel the strength of its' foundation. In the next season apostles and prophets are going to be established to not only usher in community transformation, but also to keep the harvest that the Lord intends to send. Our job is to build an infrastructure that can hold or keep the fruit that Lord desires to send. At present, the current wineskin structures of the church are not prepared. Ephesians 2:19-22 (ESV) states:

> *Now, therefore, you are no longer strangers and foreigners, but are fellow citizens with the saints and members of the household of God, having been built upon the foundation of the apostles and prophets, Jesus Christ Himself being the chief cornerstone, in whom the entire building, tightly framed together, grows into a holy temple in the Lord, in whom you also are being built together into a dwelling place of God through the Spirit.*

The second reason the Lord is aligning His government is because His Body has been employing natural means to war with a supernatural enemy.

We have been experiencing 'hell on earth' instead of 'heaven on earth' because the church has been warring with programs instead of the power of the Holy Spirit. This is why the Lord instructed us to pray in Matthew 6:9-10 (NKJV):

> *"Our Father who is in heaven, hallowed be Your name. Your kingdom come. Your will be done, on earth as it is in heaven."*

1 Corinthians 4:20 (ESV):

> *For the kingdom of God does not consist in talk but in power.*

God is restoring apostolic power and anointing to the church to set us free from the bondages that have been holding us back from fulfilling the Great Commission. When apostles, prophets, evangelists, pastors and teachers work together in unity they raise up many congregations, or families, with the same mission - to make earth like heaven!

The term 'Christian' means 'Little Christ'. The word 'Christ' means 'anointed one.' Acts 10:36-38 (ESV) tells us:

> *As for the word that he sent to Israel, preaching good news of peace through Jesus Christ (He is Lord of all), you yourselves know what happened throughout all Judea, beginning from Galilee after the baptism that John proclaimed: how God anointed Jesus of Nazareth with the Holy Spirit and with power. He went about doing good and*

healing all who were oppressed by the devil, for God was with him.

1 John 3:8 (ESV adds:

The reason the Son of God appeared was to destroy the works of the devil.

If the Son lives in and through us, shouldn't we also be doing what Jesus portrayed, as related in Acts 10:36-38 and 1 John 3:8?

Jesus said in Acts 1:8 that we would receive power to showcase Him to the world. The apostle Paul received such power on the road to Damascus (Acts 9:1-4), and lived out his life and mission accordingly:

Therefore I (Paul) have reason to glory in Christ Jesus in the things which pertain to God. For I will not dare to speak of any of those things which Christ has not accomplished through me, in word and deed, to make the Gentiles obedient— in mighty signs and wonders, by the power of the Spirit of God, so that from Jerusalem and round about to Illyricum I have fully preached the gospel of Christ. Romans 15:17-19 (NKJV)

The third reason the Lord is aligning His government is because we haven't allowed the power of the Holy Spirit into our churches to deal with the wounds that God's people and pre-believers carry.

ACE's or Adverse Childhood Experiences are traumatic incidents that young people go through up until the age of 18 that lead to long term health issues. According to a CDC-Kaiser Permanente Adverse Childhood Study there are ten types of childhood trauma:

1. A parent being incarcerated
2. A parent who dies prematurely
3. A parent verbally abusing them
4. A parent sexually abusing them
5. A parent abusing drugs and alcohol
6. A parent having mental health issues
7. A parent hitting or slapping them physically
8. Their parents getting a divorce or separation
9. Watching the father physically abuse the mother
10. Their parents not providing for the physical and emotional needs

According to the CDC-Kaiser study, other traumatic incidents also include:

- Racism
- Being bullied
- Homelessness
- Being in the foster care system for years
- Watching parents physically abuse a sibling

The same study also revealed:

- People who have had 6 or more ACE's can die earlier than those who have had none
- 67% of the populace has had at least one ACE
- 1/8 of the population has had four ACE's

So, here's the deal: Today, our society is cracking at the seams because our families are in disarray. By God's divine grace He is raising up healing and deliverance ministries to help stabilize and empower families to prosper. This is why the Lord is restoring the offices of prophet and apostle to establish His government and effect change in the earth.

What does God's government look like?
There is a fivefold function:

1. Apostles build
2. Prophets reveal
3. Evangelists gather
4. Pastors nurture
5. Teachers explain

Each office represents 1/5, or 20%, of the ministry of Jesus. When all five offices are functioning in the Body of Christ, the life-altering ministry of Jesus will operate at an optimal level.

One of the reasons why apostles and prophets are not widely accepted today is because of a religious spirit, which resists them for fear of God's revelatory insight and power returning to the church. A second reason can be attributed to the lack of Bible study.

A quick numerical study of the five offices of Jesus is revealing:

1. The term apostle is mentioned 80 times in the Bible
2. The term prophet is employed 172 times
3. The term evangelist 3 times
4. The term pastor 1 time
5. The term teacher 13 times

The bottom line is this: The offices of apostle and prophet reveal the works of the enemy in people's lives and break the spiritual barriers keeping them from fulfilling their purpose and call in Christ. How does this come about? Ephesians 4:11-16 (NKJV) makes the purposes of the five offices clear:

> *And He Himself gave some to be apostles, some prophets, some evangelists, and some pastors and teachers, for the equipping of the saints for the work of ministry, for the edifying of the body of Christ, till we all come to the unity of the faith and of the knowledge of the Son of God, to a perfect man, to the measure of the stature of the fullness of Christ; that we should no longer be children, tossed to and fro and carried about with every wind of doctrine, by the trickery of men, in the cunning craftiness of deceitful plotting, but, speaking the truth in love, may grow up in all things into Him who is the head—Christ—from whom the whole body, joined and knit together by what every joint supplies, according to the effective working by which every part does its share, causes growth of the body for the edifying of itself in love.*

Mending the Nets:

The word 'equip' is often confused with the word 'train'. 'Equip' (*katartismos* from *katartizo*) means to mend, repair, make whole or perfect and the of setting bones. 'Mending the nets' is derived from *kata* plus *artízo* meaning to adjust, fit and finish. To mend the nets means to make something or someone (in this case the 'sheep' in the flock) completely adequate or sufficient for something. The basic idea of the word is transforming a thing into the condition in which it ought to be. In politics it is used for bringing together opposing factions so that a government can function in unity.

The word 'mend' is *kat-artízō,* a compound Greek word meaning complete, perfect of its kind, suitable or exactly fitted, (Liddell & Scott). This is what a net or our heart possessed before it was torn by sin (We were exactly fitted to do what God designed us to do before the Fall). When the following two words *kat-artízō* are fitted together they mean to refit, repair and mend that which is broken. [2]

Here's my a-ha: You and I are nets that have tears in them, which need mending. Once we are mended, Jesus can throw us into the water to proclaim the goodness of God to other fish.

We are Being Prepared for a Massive Catch!
One day as Jesus was standing by the Lake of Gennesaret, the people were crowding around him and listening to the word of God. He saw at the water's edge two boats, left there by the fishermen, who were washing their nets. He got into one of the boats, the one belonging to Simon, and asked him to put out a little from shore. Then he sat down and taught the people from the boat. When he had finished speaking, he said to Simon, "Put out into deep water, and let down the nets for a catch." Simon answered, "Master, we've worked hard all night and haven't caught anything. But because you say so, I will let down the nets." When they had done so, (they caught such a large number of fish that their nets began to break). So they signaled their partners in the other boat to come and help them, and they came and filled both boats so full that they began to sink. and so were James and John, the sons of Zebedee, Simon's partners. Then Jesus said to Simon, "Don't be afraid; from now on you will fish for people." For he and all his

companions were astonished at the catch of fish they had taken, When Simon Peter saw this, he fell at Jesus' knees and said, "Go away from me, Lord; I am a sinful man!" So they pulled their boats up on shore, left everything and followed him. Luke 5:1-11 (NIV)

The nets broke after Jesus summoned a great catch of fish. Why? Because these young apostles in the making were not yet equipped to be fishers of men. Like us, the Lord had to cleanse them first. This begs the question, did Jesus equip or clean up His disciples?

John 15:1-5 ESV provides the answer:

I am the true vine, and my Father is the vinedresser. Every branch in me that does not bear fruit he takes away, and every branch that does bear fruit he prunes, that it may bear more fruit. Already you are clean because of the word that I have spoken to you. Abide in me, and I in you. As the branch cannot bear fruit by itself, unless it abides in the vine, neither can you, unless you abide in me. I am the vine; you are the branches. Whoever abides in me and I in him, he it is that bears much fruit, for apart from me you can do nothing.

The Greek word for 'clean' is *katharos*. Used 27 times in the New Testament it means, pure, unsoiled, cleansed from guilt, innocent and void of evil.[3] We don't know what word Jesus spoke or declared over His disciples, but it was so powerful that they were cleansed from guilt.

Three Years Later:
John 21:10-11 (ESV):

Jesus said to them, "Bring some of the fish you have just caught." So Simon Peter climbed back into the boat and dragged the net ashore. It was full of large fish, 153, but even with so many (the net was not torn).

Unlike Luke 5:1-11, the nets did not tear because the disciples had been 'equipped' by Jesus. How many great men of God have lost their ministries because they were not set free from personal strongholds? How many individuals are no longer walking with God because they concluded if this is Christianity, we want nothing to do with it?

If we want to finish the race set before us by God, we need to emphasize the vital importance of equipping the Body of Christ through inner healing, deliverance and generational deliverance ministries. I believe that John 21:10-11 is a prophetic glimpse of the ingathering of human souls that is coming, because the number 153 means, "I am God!" If we are equipped (strengthened and healed), like surfers to ride big waves, we will rip on the surge of revival waters headed our way. But, if we do not get equipped, we will surely slip off our boards and not be able to withstand the POWER that's coming.

Training for Reigning:
But solid food is for the mature, for those who have their powers of discernment trained by constant practice to distinguish good from evil. Hebrews 5:14 (ESV)

The Greek word for training is *hexis* and is only used once in the entire New Testament. Interestingly, this verse ties training to a believer who is mature and is learning to discern between good and evil. Ephesians 4:11-14 (ESV) reminds us that when the fivefold officers of the church equip the family of God, the result is unity, intimacy and maturity.

> *And he gave the apostles, the prophets, the evangelists, the shepherds and teachers, to equip the saints for the work of ministry, for building up the body of Christ, until we all attain to the unity of the faith and of the knowledge of the Son of God, to mature manhood, to the measure of the stature of the fullness of Christ, so that we may no longer be children, tossed to and fro by the waves and carried about by every wind of doctrine, by human cunning, by craftiness in deceitful schemes.*

Mending our nets is not enough to advance the Gospel of the kingdom. We also need to train and empower the Body of the Lord to make tangible marketplace and community impact.

The Rabbinic Method (observe, model, practice):
Jesus was a rabbi (Mark 9:5; 10:51) and employed the 'Rabbinic Method' to train His disciples for kingdom service. First, He selected 12 men to pour His life into and then He spent every day for the next three years, preparing them to transform the world. The key word here is 'spent.' Jesus spent time with His disciples, in stark contrast to the discipleship methods we employ today.

During His three-year ministry Jesus' spiritual sons and daughters witnessed how much He loved broken people (Matthew 9:36). To download His heart for the Lost, Jesus regularly demonstrated what divine grace-filled compassion looked like by healing the sick and delivering the demonized from debilitating bondages. He did not debate or teach like the Pharisees or Greek philosophers of his day but demonstrated how to flow in the power of the

Holy Spirit by healing the sick and casting out demons. Jesus implemented live on-the-spot training times for His disciples (Luke 10:1-9, 17), which reproduced kingdom ministry in those who followed after Him. Let's look at four examples – Peter, Stephen, Philipp, Paul.

Peter - Acts 5:12-16 (ESV):

> *Now many signs and wonders were regularly done among the people by the hands of the apostles. And they were all together in Solomon's Portico. None of the rest dared join them, but the people held them in high esteem. And more than ever believers were added to the Lord, multitudes of both men and women, so that they even carried out the sick into the streets and laid them on cots and mats, that as Peter came by at least his shadow might fall on some of them. The people also gathered from the towns around Jerusalem, bringing the sick and those afflicted with unclean spirits, and they were all healed.*
>
> *Now as Peter went here and there among them all, he came down also to the saints who lived at Lydda. There he found a man named Aeneas, bedridden for eight years, who was paralyzed. And Peter said to him, "Aeneas, Jesus Christ heals you; rise and make your bed." And immediately he rose. And all the residents of Lydda and Sharon saw him, and they turned to the Lord. Acts 9:32-35 (ESV)*

Stephen - Acts 6:8 (ESV):

> *And Stephen, full of grace and power, was doing great wonders and signs among the people.*

Philipp - Acts 8:4-8 (ESV):

> *Now those who were scattered went about preaching the word. Philip went down to the city of Samaria and proclaimed to them the Christ. And the crowds with one accord paid attention to what was being said by Philip, when they heard him and saw the signs that he did. For unclean spirits, crying out with a loud voice, came out of many who had them, and many who were paralyzed or lame were healed. So there was much joy in that city.*

Note: The most exciting thing about Stephen and Philip's ministry is that they were not apostles or other fivefold officers. They were kingdom practicing believers who had observed and learned the Jesus/Rabbinic way of ministering to people.

Paul - Acts 14:8-10 and 19:11-12 (ESV):

> *Now at Lystra there was a man sitting who could not use his feet. He was crippled from birth and had never walked. He listened to Paul speaking. And Paul, looking intently at him and seeing that he had faith to be made well, said in a loud voice, "Stand upright on your feet." And he sprang up and began walking.*

> *And God was doing extraordinary miracles by the hands of Paul, so that even handkerchiefs or aprons that had touched his skin were carried away to the sick, and their diseases left them and the evil spirits came out of them.*

The Gospel of the Kingdom:
For years, I presented the Gospel of Jesus Christ to pre-believers with not much fruit, employing evangelistic tracts

like the *Four Spiritual Laws*, the 'Roman Road', and *Steps to Peace with God*. But in the past decade, the Holy Spirit has added a kingdom dimension when interacting with non-believers. Let me explain. In Matthew 4:23-25 (ESV), Jesus proclaimed the gospel of the kingdom among the people:

> *And he went throughout all Galilee, teaching in their synagogues and proclaiming the gospel of the kingdom and healing every disease and every affliction among the people. So his fame spread throughout all Syria, and they brought him all the sick, those afflicted with various diseases and pains, those oppressed by demons, those having seizures, and paralytics, and he healed them. And great crowds followed him from Galilee and the Decapolis, and from Jerusalem and Judea, and from beyond the Jordan.*

Matthew 24:10, 9-14:

> *And then many will fall away and betray one another and hate one another. Then they will deliver you up to tribulation and put you to death, and you will be hated by all nations for my name's sake. And many false prophets will arise and lead many astray. And because lawlessness will be increased, the love of many will grow cold. But the one who endures to the end will be saved. <u>And this gospel of the kingdom</u> will be proclaimed throughout the whole world as a testimony to all nations, and then the end will come.*

A Tongan Woman's Conversion:
Recruited by a home care agency to take care of my 94-year-old mother a tall, intimidating looking Tongan woman stood in front of me at our front door. "Oh boy", I thought

to myself, working with this caregiver is going to be challenging.

In the weeks that followed I did my best to get to know this woman in-spite of my fear of her stature. One evening as I was preparing dinner, the Holy Spirit whispered something that I thought could not be possibly true. I heard, "She comes from royal blood." Stepping out by faith and obedience I asked her, "Do you come from royal blood?" Stunned she looked at me and replied, "How do you know that?" I replied, "God told me; and He wants to reveal Himself to you."

Still stunned, my mother's caregiver asked me two more times how I knew that she came from royal blood. Again, I told her that Jesus was trying to get her attention. I then asked, "Is it true? Do you have royal blood?" She answered, "My father was the former President of Tonga."

I then felt, through discernment, pain in the middle of my spine so I asked her if she had such an issue. Stunned once again she blurted, "How do you know that? Only my doctor and I know about this! How do you know that?" Like before, I told her that God was revealing Himself to her. Then the Holy Spirit revealed one more thing as I felt pain in my eye, so I asked if she was having issues with her right eye. One more time she queried, "How do you know that?"

Well, as you might imagine after three supernatural insights like this she was open to the Gospel and received Jesus as her Lord and Savior. I then led her to receive the baptism of the Holy Spirit, and she was on cloud nine. Just when I thought the Lord was finished, she said, "I can't believe it, my eye is healed!"

This was the most powerful evangelistic encounter I have ever been a part of! This was the Gospel of the kingdom (1 Corinthians 4:20)! My heart is to train a generation of hungry believers how to move with the Holy Spirit so the Gospel of the kingdom can be taken to every nation.

In Chapter Seven I'm going to share 18 reasons why God's healing power is siphoned off from healing the sick.

---

[1] This is a graphical depiction of Diffusion of Innovations (1962), a model created by Ohio State professor Everett Rogers as a method of explaining how, why, and the rate at which an innovation spreads through a population or social system.

[2] Complete Word Study Dictionary: NT

[3] *Mounce Greek Dictionary*

CHAPTER SEVEN:
EIGHTEEN REASONS WHY PEOPLE DON'T GET HEALED
ROB GROSS

1. **They Don't Obey God's Word (laws, statutes, rules etc.):**

   And he cried to the Lord, and the Lord showed him a log, and he threw it into the water, and the water became sweet. There the Lord made for them a statute and a rule, and there he tested them, Then Moses made Israel set out from the Red Sea, and they went into the wilderness of Shur. They went three days in the wilderness and found no water. When they came to Marah, they could not drink the water of Marah because it was bitter; therefore it was named Marah. And the people grumbled against Moses, saying, "What shall we drink?" saying, "If you will diligently listen to the voice of the Lord your God, and do that which is right in his eyes, and give ear to his commandments and keep all his statutes, I will put none of the diseases on you that I put on the Egyptians, for I am the Lord, your healer." Exodus 15:22-26 (ESV)

   This passage is clear. If we obey God's Word, He promises to protect us from infirmity and disease. This passage raises the question then, "Where have we not obeyed God's Word?" The question requires honest reflection. Ponder the following questions: 1) Have you forgiven everyone who has hurt you or are you still bitter (Ephesians 4:31)? 2) Have you faithfully paid all your taxes (Mathew 22:22)?

2.They Do Not Ask the Elders of their Church to Pray for Them:

> *You do not have because you do not ask. James 4:2b (ESV)*

> *Is anyone among you suffering? Let him pray. Is anyone cheerful? Let him sing praise. Is anyone among you sick? <u>Let him call for the elders of the church, and let them pray over him, anointing him with oil in the name of the Lord. And the prayer of faith will save the one who is sick, and the Lord will raise him up</u>. And if he has committed sins, he will be forgiven. James 5:13-15 (ESV)*

Testimony:

In my opinion, one of the most overlooked passages in the Bible is James 5:13-15. These three verses clearly state that if a member of a local church is sick, they can call the elders of their church to pray for them by faith and **they will be healed.**

In 2023, the elders of our church were asked by the husband of a stage 4 cancer patient to pray for his wife. The elders gladly responded and visited his wife in their home, anointed her with oil and asked the Lord to heal her.

I called this precious woman later to see how she was doing, and she told me that she was pressing into God and continuing to declare that she was healed. I responded by reminding her what James 5:13-15 stated and encouraged her instead to respectfully remind the Lord about His promise to heal her if the elders prayed over her by faith.

Ongoing prayer is powerful but resting by faith in the declared promises of God, is even more powerful. In Psalm 46:10 King David, under the inspiration of the Holy Spirit declared, *"Cease striving and know that I am God."* I love this verse because it reminds me that God is in total control of my life situation at any time and because He is I don't need to strive to get Him to hear or answer my prayers.

I'm sure you're wondering right now what happened to the cancer patient. The cancer has shrunk. She is still resting in the Lord (trusting Him) to restore her completely.

3.Unconfessed Sin:

> *He who covers his sins will not prosper <u>but whoever confesses and forsakes</u> them will have mercy. Proverbs 28:13 (ESV)*

> *<u>Therefore, confess your sins to one another and pray for one another, that you may be healed.</u> The prayer of a righteous person has great power as it is working. James 5:16-17 (ESV)*

> *<u>I</u>f we confess our sins, he is faithful and just to forgive us our sins and to cleanse us from all unrighteousness. 1 John 1:9 (ESV)*

The Greek word for confession is *homolegeo,* meaning 'to admit, agree with or confess.' When we cover or hide our sins, Proverbs 28:13 clearly states that we will not prosper! But, if we admit our sins to God and confess them to other believers (and forsake them), the Lord will mercifully heal us.

God has committed Himself in His faithfulness and justice to forgive and to cleanse us if we agree with Him that we have sinned or 'missed the mark.' But fessing up to God and others is easier said than done because of our pride and fear of rejection. In 1 Peter 5:5b (ESV), the Lord issues a stern warning for us to heed:

Clothe yourselves, all of you, with humility toward one another, for "God opposes the proud but gives grace to the humble."

Throughout the Bible we see examples where individuals hid their sins from God. Such was the case when David lay with Bathsheba and tried to cover up her pregnancy by having her husband killed in battle. Refusing to admit the heinous nature of his sin, David suffered immensely:

Blessed is the one whose transgression is forgiven, whose sin is covered. Blessed is the man against whom the Lord counts no iniquity, and in whose spirit there is no deceit. For when I kept silent, my bones wasted away through my groaning all day long. For day and night your hand was heavy upon me; my strength was dried up as by the heat of summer. Psalm 32:1-4 (ESV)

2 Samuel 12 tells us that David paid a heavy price for covering up his sin, including the loss of his infant son. But Psalm 32:5-7 (ESV) reveals that when David confessed his sin, God cleansed him:

I acknowledged my sin to you, and I did not cover my iniquity; I said, "I will confess my transgressions to the Lord," and you forgave the iniquity of my sin. Therefore let everyone who is godly offer prayer to you at a time when you may be found; surely in the rush of great waters, they shall not reach him. You are a hiding place for me; you preserve me from trouble; you surround me with shouts of deliverance.

Do you have any hidden or unconfessed sins you need to confess?

A Prayer to Repent for Hiding Your Sins:

Father, please forgive me for hiding my sins from You, others and myself. I acknowledge now, that I have foolishly believed that You have not been aware of what I have done and continue to do to the present day. Lord, I admit now out of a repentant heart that I have broken Your heart, hurt others and hurt myself by not living according to Your Word (1 John 1:9). I confess that I have rebelled against You and ask not only for You to forgive me, but to cleanse me of all unrighteousness as repent for and renounce my sins (name them specifically). Create a clean heart within me Lord and restore the joy of my salvation. In Jesus name, amen.

4.Unbelief:

And he could do no mighty work there, except that he laid his hands on a few sick people and healed them. And he marveled because of their unbelief. And he went about among the villages teaching. Mark 6:5-6 (ESV)

See to it, brothers and sisters, that none of you has a sinful, unbelieving heart that turns away from the living God. But encourage one another daily, as long as it is called "Today," so that none of you may be hardened by sin's deceitfulness. Hebrews 3:12-13 NIV

A Sad Story:

In 1996, while serving as a prayer minister at a healing ministry in Honolulu, a woman brought her daughter to be prayed over because she still could not walk at the age of 3. One of the prayer ministers asked the mother if she believed Jesus could heal her daughter and strangely, she said, "No."

The prayer minister asked why and she shared that she did not believe in divine healing, but her mother did (the little girl's grandmother) and she brought her daughter at her request.

A decade later this same mother and her daughter visited our church, and her daughter could still not walk. So sad!

A Prayer to Renounce Unbelief

Oh God, we come to you in Jesus' name, and we confess our sin of unbelief. We do not try to excuse it. We are responsible for it. We are sorry for it. We ask you to forgive us and to deliver us from it and impart to us your faith. And tonight, we want to declare each of us individually, I believe in God the Father; I believe in Jesus Christ, His Son; I believe in God the Holy Spirit, and I believe in the Bible, the true authoritative Word of God. I believe Lord Jesus what you said: God's Word is the truth. Amen.[1]

5. Past Involvement in Cults and False Religions (Generationally and Personally)

Do not bow down before their gods or worship them or follow their practices. You must demolish them and break their sacred stones to pieces. Worship the Lord your God, and his blessing will be on your food and water. I will take away sickness from among you, and none will miscarry or be barren in your land. I will give you a full life span. Exodus 23:24-26 (NIV)

Freemasonry is a successor of the ancient mysteries religions: the secret worship rites of pagan gods such as Allah, Baal, Lucifer and Osiris to name a few.

In 1998, I prayed for a woman who had stage 4 brain cancer. While interviewing her I asked her if she had been involved with Freemasonry. She replied no but shared that her father was a 33rd degree Freemason. I responded by having her pray a lengthy prayer to break free from Freemasonry. Later that year I received an email from someone notifying me that her brain cancer had completely disappeared!

Years later the mother of a 17-year-old son sought council as to why her son was dealing with a wide assortment of skin diseases and other ailments. Her husband came from an English family, so I asked her if he or any of his family members had been involved with the Freemasons. Her husband acknowledged that Freemasonry was in his family, but when he consulted his pastor to see if his son's ailments were connected to Freemasonry, the pastor told him to disregard the possibility. Three years later this couple's son died mysteriously in his sleep at the age of twenty. I have often wondered if they (the father and mother) had cut ties with Freemasonry, their son would still be alive?

An adaptation of an original *Prayer of Release for Masons and Their Descendants* is recommended, and can be accessed at https://aslansplace.com/language/en/prayer-of-release-for-masons-and-their-descendants/

6. Spirits of Pain and Infirmity are Not Expelled

> *Now when the sun was setting, all those who had anyone sick with various diseases brought them to Him and He laid His hands on every one of them and healed them. And demons or evil spirits also came out of many crying out. Luke 4:40-41 (ESV)*

> *On a Sabbath Jesus was teaching in one of the synagogues, and a woman was there who had been*

*crippled (disabled) by a spirit for eighteen years.
She was bent over and could not straighten up at
all. When Jesus saw her, he called her forward and
said to her, "Woman, you are set free from your
infirmity." Then he put his hands on her, and
immediately she straightened up and praised God.*
Luke 13:10-13 (NIV)

Some physical issues are not healed because there is a
demonic root that has not been dealt with. Please know that
I am not suggesting that all physical diseases are
demonically induced but can be tied to the Netherworld in
certain instances.

Testimony:
While teaching a class on a Sunday afternoon at my office
the Lord showed me that someone in the class was dealing
with arthritis. I called out the condition and a woman in her
mid 40's raised her had to acknowledge that she had this
debilitating disease. I proceeded to ask her if she or anyone
in her family had refused to forgive others for past offenses.
She nodded yes, so I led her in a prayer of repentance.

Seconds after she had renounced holding onto past hurts on
behalf of her family and herself, the Holy Spirit came upon
her knocking her down to the floor on her knees screaming
in pain. Looking closer, her entire hand had contorted as the
Lord was flushing out the spirit of arthritis in her hand. This
display of divine power lasted another minute until the
woman's hand went limp.

15 years later I bumped into this woman and asked her if
she was arthritis free. With a smile on her face, she said that
she still no longer suffered from the awful pain that had
plagued her hand. PTL!

Another Testimony:
During a ministry time on a Sunday morning, I walked to the back of the church sanctuary to check up on our prayer team as they prayed for multiple people needing healing prayer. As I walked by a woman being prayed over for severe back pain, I heard the Lord say, "Command the spirits of pain and infirmity to leave." In response to the Lord's leading, I did what He told me to do and the woman crumpled to the floor. A week later I received a text from the woman informing that her back was healed!

7. Past Involvement in Occult Practice

> *There shall not be found among you anyone who makes his son or his daughter pass through the fire, one who uses <u>divination</u>, one who practices <u>witchcraft</u>, or one who interprets omens, or a sorcerer, or one who casts a spell, or a medium, or a spiritist, or one who calls up the dead. For whoever does these things is detestable to the Lord; and because of these detestable things the Lord your God will drive them out before you.* Deuteronomy 18:10-12 (ESV)

> *Do not turn to mediums or spiritists; <u>do not seek them out to be defiled by them</u>. I am the Lord your God.* Leviticus 19:31(NASB)

Such evil includes:

- Tarot card reading
- Fortunetelling
- Horoscopes
- Ouija Board

- Seances
- Spiritism
- Voodoo

A Prayer to Renounce The Occult

Lord, if I have ever been involved in the occult, even ignorantly, whatever it was, I confess it as sin and renounce it. I ask you to forgive me and I commit myself now that never again will I be involved in those things. Forgive me, Lord, and release me from their influence, right now. In the name of Jesus, Amen. [2]

8. Generational Curses Not Brought to Death on the Cross

"You shall not make for yourself a carved image, or any likeness of anything that is in heaven above, or that is in the earth beneath, or that is in the water under the earth. You shall not bow down to them or serve them, for I the Lord your God am a jealous God, visiting the iniquity of the fathers on the children to the third and the fourth generation of those who hate me, but showing steadfast love to thousands of those who love me and keep my commandments. Exodus 20:4-6 (ESV)

Joshua laid an oath on them at that time, saying, "Cursed before the Lord be the man who rises up and rebuilds this city, Jericho." At the cost of his firstborn shall he lay its foundation, and at the cost of his youngest son shall he set up its gates." Joshua 6:26 (ESV)

In Ahab's time, Hiel of Bethel rebuilt Jericho. He laid its foundations at the cost of his firstborn son

Abiram, and he set up its gates at the cost of his youngest son Segub, in accordance with the word of the Lord spoken by Joshua son of Nun. 1 Kings 16:34 (NIV)

What is a curse?

First, a curse is **a warning of the consequences** that will come about if God's command is broken. For example, God warned Adam and Eve that If they ate of the fruit of the tree of the knowledge of good and evil, they would die.

Second, the curse speaks about **the consequences and punishment of sin**. It speaks about the binding power of the curse that limits the life and productivity of the one who is cursed. The person is bound and unable to accomplish what he or she was once able to do.

Third, the curse is **a withdrawal of the blessing of God**, It is the blessing of God that brings freedom, peace, increase, and plenty. The curse speaks of reduction in every area of life. We can make a lot of money, but it is never enough. We can do things that should bring success, but it is always elusive.

A Word of Caution:

Don't fix your eyes on the demonic. Fix your eyes on Jesus! As the Lord removes the demonic (curses, past cult involvement, the occult) off of you, you will steadily receive the 'fullness' of God's blessings in your life.

Seven Indicators of a Curse:

Derek Prince says that the effects of being under a curse can be summarized in one word, 'frustration'. We may have great outward success but there is inward frustration, relationships that are in chaos, peace always seems to elude us.

Prince compiled the following list of seven indicators that a curse is at work in a person's life. Go ahead and review the list. If only two or three apply, that may not indicate a curse, unless they repeatedly take place on a regular basis.

- Being accident prone
- Ongoing financial insufficiency
- Mental and/or emotional breakdown
- Breakdown of marriage and family alienation
- A history of suicide and unnatural or untimely deaths
- Repeated chronic sicknesses (especially if hereditary)
- Barrenness, a tendency to miscarry or related female problems

The Kennedy Curse:
Some believe that the "Kennedy curse" began when the patriarch of the family, Joseph P. Kennedy Sr., refused Rabbi Aharon Kotler's request to help save European Jews from certain death at the hands of the Nazis. Some say that Rabbi Kotler asked Kennedy to let in a boat full of Jews to the US, the *SS St. Louis*, and when Kennedy refused, the boat was forced to return to Nazi Europe where all the Jews died. The story goes that not only did Kennedy refuse to help but he was rude to the rabbi and publicly humiliated him. The rabbi subsequently cursed him that his family would suffer from a series of unnatural deaths - *misa meshuna*, which is the Talmudic term for an unnatural death - a life cut short due to an accident or other unfortunate event rather than a natural death from old age.

I'm of the opinion that Genesis 12:3 was activated when Joseph Kennedy Sr. refused to bless the Jews and as a result Joe Jr, JFK, JFK Jr and Robert Kennedy all died prematurely.

9. Unforgiveness:

> *If I regard wickedness in my heart, the Lord will not hear [my prayer].* Psalm 66:18-19 (NKJV)

> *And whenever you stand praying, forgive, if you have anything against anyone, so that your Father also who is in heaven may forgive you your trespasses."* Mark 11:26 (ESV)

> *And do not grieve the Holy Spirit of God, by whom you were sealed for the day of redemption. Let all bitterness and wrath and anger and clamor and slander be put away from you, along with all malice. Be kind to one another, tenderhearted, forgiving one another, as God in Christ forgave you.* Ephesians 4:30-32 (ESV)

Jesus said before you start to pray, check your heart by asking: Is there anyone I'm holding bitterness against or have not forgiven in my heart?

Why did Jesus say this? If we pray with resentment and unforgiveness in our hearts, the resentment and unforgiveness will be barriers that hinder our prayers from being answered.

A Prayer to Forgive those Who Have Hurt You:

Holy Spirit, I ask you now in Jesus' name, speak to my heart and show me if there are areas of bitterness, resentment and unforgiveness towards anyone. Lord, if there has been any resentment in my heart, any unforgiveness, any bitterness, I renounce it now. I lay it down. For those who have harmed me, or wronged me, I forgive them now, as

I would have You forgive me. Lord, I forgive them, and I believe you have forgiven me. Thank You, Lord, in Jesus' name.

10.Ungodly Belief Systems:

I don't deserve to be healed by God because I've done too many bad things:

> *The Lord God took the man and put him in the garden of Eden to work it and keep it. And the Lord God commanded the man, saying, "You may surely eat of every tree of the garden, but of the tree of the knowledge of good and evil you shall not eat, for in the day that you eat of it you shall surely die."* Genesis 2:15-17 (ESV)

> *So when the woman saw that the tree was good for food, and that it was a delight to the eyes, and that the tree was to be desired to make one wise, she took of its fruit and ate, and she also gave some to her husband who was with her, and he ate. Then the eyes of both were opened, and they knew that they were naked. And they sewed fig leaves together and made themselves loincloths. And they heard the sound of the Lord God walking in the garden in the cool of the day, and the man and his wife hid themselves from the presence of the Lord God among the trees of the garden. And he said, "I heard the sound of you in the garden, and I was afraid, because I was naked, and I hid myself." But the Lord God called to the man and said to him, "Where are you?"* Genesis 3:6-10 (ESV)

The Tree of Knowledge of Good and Evil:
In Genesis 3:6 Eve was seduced by the wisdom (human reasoning) she could gain by eating from the tree of

knowledge and good and evil. Succumbing to temptation she picked its' fruit, ate and shared it with Adam. In a millisecond, the mother and father of the human race were radically torn from the Father's embrace and became wise in their own eyes (not to mention becoming fearful and covering up their nakedness or shame). Because of Adam and Eve's fall in the Garden of Eden, our thoughts, beliefs and speech patterns are tied to the roots of the tree of knowledge and good and evil.

Paul Cox's 'Aha!'

In a February 2022 seminar, my colleague unpacked revelation from the Lord that has revolutionized my thinking. The roots, trunk, branches, leaves and fruit of the tree of knowledge of good and evil are unbiblical mindsets or belief systems tied to our carnal nature. For physical healing to take place, our ungodly belief systems rooted in the tree of knowledge of good and evil must be dealt with by bringing them to death on the cross (by confessing, repenting, renouncing and changing what we say, believe and think about God's ability to heal us, our attitude while going through adversity and our response to others who have hurt or offended us).

Breaking free from deeply ingrained negative self-talk is not easy and requires a transformational process referred to in Romans 12:2 as, "the renewal of the mind." I met over a year ago with a husband and wife for dinner. The husband had just been given a serious cancer diagnosis and were, of course, very frightened.

Prior to having dinner with them, the Lord downloaded into my spirit a negative mindset that the man's wife was struggling with. During dinner I broached the possibility that although she believed that God could and does heal today, she believed that He did not want to heal her husband. Her mindset traced back 25 years earlier when her son fell ill, and the Lord did not heal him in-spite of her prayers. When her son tragically died, she believed two lies: 1) That the Lord did not hear her prayers and 2) that although the Lord could heal anyone, He would not heal the members of her family. She brought these lies to death on the cross and today her husband is cancer free!

Genesis 3:6 explains why our belief systems are so difficult to break free from. In verse 6 Eve coveted the wisdom (human reasoning) she believed she would gain by eating from the tree of knowledge and good and evil. In a catastrophic moment of folly she took its' fruit, ate it and shared it with Adam. In that moment when Adam and Eve were torn out of the Father's embrace, they started doing life through their own strength and wisdom.

When we come to faith in Christ we are disconnected from the tree of knowledge of good and evil and reconnected to the tree of life. Jesus is the tree of Life! Proverbs 3:18 screams (my paraphrase here), "Wisdom is a tree of life." Revelation 22:1-3 (NKJV) shouts:

> *"And he showed me a pure river of water of life, clear as crystal, proceeding from the throne of God and of the Lamb. In the middle of its street, and on either side of the river, was the tree of life, which bore twelve fruits, each tree yielding its fruit every month. <u>The leaves of the tree were for the healing of the nations.</u>"*

If we commit ourselves to continually renew our minds with God's wisdom and blueprint for living, we will live healthy lives. If our thinking, however, is rooted in the tree of knowledge of good and evil we will succumb to the spirit of stupidity (Proverbs 5:23).

Some in need of a divine breakthrough will attend a healing service hoping God will heal them. But what if they aren't aligned with God's wisdom when they arrive? What if they have thoughts like, "God doesn't really heal today, does He?" Such thoughts are like endless time loops or false scripts playing over and over in our heads. God wants to heal us, but He cannot do so because our thinking is rooted in the wrong tree.

Proverbs 23:7 (KJV) declares:

As a man thinks in his heart so is he.

So, I submit to you that for us to be physically healed the Lord wants us to deal with our belief systems: what we believe about His ability to heal us, how we think during seasons of adversity, what we declare about ourselves, what we think and say about others, what we believe about the goodness of God and much more.

Which Tree are Your Thoughts Rooted in?
I believe the roots of the tree of knowledge of good and evil are the false wisdom (being wise in our own eyes) that Adam and Eve passed down to us.

Examples of Ungodly Beliefs:
- I hate myself!
- I'm not going to live.
- God doesn't love me.
- God doesn't heal today.
- I am unworthy to be healed.
- I'm the black sheep of my family.
- Miracles are the exception, not the rule.
- I will never forgive he or she for hurting me.

- I've done too many bad things for God to forgive me.
- I believe God heals others, but not me or the members of my family.
- God is using my sickness to teach me a lesson and share in the sufferings of Christ.

A Prayer to Disconnect from the Tree of Knowledge of Good and Evil

Father, I ask You to disconnect any parts of my mind, will or emotions that are still connected to the tree of knowledge of good and evil. I commit myself today, Lord, to read Your Word on a daily basis so that my mind, will and emotions are steadily transformed into Your heart, nature and likeness. My desire Lord, is to think like You think, choose like You choose, and love like You love.

Please reveal to me today and in the coming weeks, where my belief systems do not align with Your Word so I can repent for and renounce them in Jesus Name. I now bring to death on Your cross every root, branch and leaf (belief system) that has been blocking my healing. This includes every lie that I have believed is true and every declaration I have spoken over myself and others. I pray all of this in the mighty Name of Jesus. Amen

Tree of Life Scriptures & Notes:

Genesis 2:8-9 NKJV: *The Lord God planted a garden eastward in Eden, and there He put the man whom He had formed. And out of the ground the Lord God made every tree grow that is pleasant to the sight and good for food. The tree of life was also in the midst of the garden, and the tree of the knowledge of good and evil.*

Genesis 3:6-7 NKJV: *So when the woman saw that the tree was good for food, that it was pleasant to the eyes, and a tree desirable to make one wise, she took of its fruit and ate. She also gave to her husband with her, and he ate. Then the eyes of both of them were opened, and they knew that they were naked; and they sewed fig leaves together and made themselves coverings.*

Proverbs 3:18 (ESV): *She (Wisdom) is a tree of life...*

Proverbs 11:30 (ESV): **...the fruit of the righteous is a tree of life.**

Proverbs 13:12 ESV: *... a desire fulfilled is a tree of life.*

Proverbs 15:4 ESV: **A gentle tongue is a tree of life.**

Revelation 22:1-2 NKJV: *And he showed me a pure river of water of life, clear as crystal, proceeding from the throne of God and of the Lamb. In the middle of its street, and on either side of the river, was the tree of life, which bore twelve fruits, each tree yielding its fruit every month. The leaves of the tree were for the household healing of the nations.*

In Revelation 22:1-2 we are told that the leaves of the tree of life are for the healing of the nations. If we re-acquaint ourselves with the vital role a leaf plays in the process of photosynthesis, we will recall that photosynthesis is the major source of oxygen that is breathed by humans and other animals.

The roots of the tree of knowledge of good and evil are the ungodly belief systems that we have when we are connected to it.

Thus, the leaves (God's Word, wisdom and Holy Spirit breathed prophetic utterances) of the tree of life are for the household healing of nations.

11) Dysfunctional Thinking

Jesus asked a paralyzed man in John 5:7, "Do you want to be healed?" Why did Jesus pose such an awkward question? Omniscient, He obviously knew the answer; secondly, He knew that His inquiry might be taken offensively. So why did He ask? Those who suffer from chronic illnesses and long-term disabilities can become so dependent upon the care and attention that they are receiving from others that they don't want to be healed. Sometimes the need for attention and someone to talk to outweighs a person's desire to be well.

12) The Refusal to See Medicine as a Way that God Heals

> *Every good gift and every perfect gift is from above, coming down from the Father of lights, with whom there is no variation or shadow due to change. James 1:17 (ESV)*

Prayer for healing and medical care should both be pursued. To think that there is only one way for you to be healed is to limit what God can do for you. God may choose to employ multiple avenues for your healing. Whether through supernatural prayer, deliverance ministry, medical treatment or a change in diet and daily activity, nothing is impossible for God!

13) Unbiblical Theology

> *Truly the signs of an apostle were accomplished among you with all perseverance, in signs and wonders and mighty deeds.* 2 Corinthians 12:12 (NKJV)

Some people cannot be healed because they believe God's healing ministry ceased to function when the First Century apostles died. These are Cessationists. They believe that the Church is in another dispensation where miraculous healings no longer occur. When your theology does not allow for divine healing, God's healing power will not flow.

To break free from the stronghold of Cessationism, repent of and renounce the following sins starting with the Old Testament time period, and moving on to the present:

Old Testament:
I repent for and renounce:

- Adam and Eve's desire to be like God and eating from the Tree of the Knowledge of Good and Evil, believing God's Word wasn't true.
- For man's building of the Tower of Babel, and man's choice to create his own religious way to God, which the Tower represented.
- For the worship of the Golden Calf (Baal/Satan) while Moses was on the mountain receiving God's commands.

- For mankind choosing to worship according to their own customs and will, rather than by obeying God's commands and statutes.

- For the slow devaluation of the Word of the Lord, as evidenced by the loss of the written Word of God until its discovery in Josiah's time.

- For the persecution and murder of the prophets of the Most High God, who moved in the miraculous, by those who claimed to worship God.

- For the Maccabean Jews' acceptance that the dead minor prophets' miracles were "more miraculous" than the prophetic words and miracles occurring in their time, and so they: Stopped expecting or believing that miracles or prophecy could be for them; turned from prophecy and relationship with God to allow only the study of the written Torah, and it's interpretation; honored what they could control (studies) and devalued what they could not control; accepted the cessation of miracles and prophecy.

- For the monumental influence of Plato's Dualistic world view which taught that the spiritual realm is superior to the natural and physical realm, which is inferior, worthless, and even evil.

- For the crucial effect Plato's writings had on the course of Church History. His writings devalued the human body, which Jesus came to save and to heal, and denied any healing ministry.

Early Church:
I repent for and renounce:

- For Maximilla declaring "After me there will be no more prophecy to the end of the age."

- For Victorian's statement that "The mighty signs and wonders of the apostles overcame the unbelievers. After that, the faith was established, the charismata have ceased, and now the church is comforted by the interpreted scripture."

- For Ambrosiaster's teachings that only Apostles can perform miracles and miracles have therefore ceased.

- For the Unscriptural Teachings of John Chrysostom (347-407) saying that: Miracles are for those weak in faith; when True Religion took hold, miracles ceased; to suffer for Christ is much greater than to experience miraculous deliverance from that suffering; the sign greater than all signs is deliverance from sin, "therefore, we don't need any other sign or miracle; if we choose Christian love as the best spiritual gift we shall have no need of signs."

- We repent for Jerome, while translating the Vulgate Bible, choosing to translate the Greek verb *sozo*, which means saved healed and delivered, as saved only, hiding the healing aspect of the verb.

- We repent for Augustine's early teachings: that miracles do not need to continue, because they will weaken faith, and keep people from maturing; his many books devaluing the miraculous, which greatly impacted the reformers centuries later; his dependence on Plato's philosophy, and not adhering only to the Word of God, and the Spirit of Truth; and, for his teachings that changed the world view of the Church from a scriptural Warfare World View to a more passive Blueprint World View.

Middle Age:

I repent for and renounce:

- All influence into Christianity from Gnosticism, especially the teaching that our bodies are evil, and that Jesus did not die on the cross and provide forgiveness for our sins and healing for our diseases.
- For the influence of Plato's Dualistic world view on the Gnostics, who then influenced the Church.
- For Gregory the Great, who said that miracles were necessary at first, but are no longer needed, thus further stifling ordinary believers from using their gifts.
- For Thomas Aquinas's, statement that the only purpose for miracles was to serve as a visible sign, a testimony to guarantee the divine source and truth of Christian Doctrine, and that enough miracles had been done to prove faith once and for all.
- That the Church Fathers who failed to see the compassion and care of our Father in the healing of the sick, and His great mercy toward the afflicted.
- For the belief of the Church Fathers that: the Apostolic level of the miraculous could not and should not be approached or attempted any longer, as it has ceased; miracles are given out by merit. No one now is righteous enough; miracles are not needed; they have been replaced by piety and the study of scripture.
- For each way these doctrines limited and grieved the Holy Spirit, throughout the centuries.
- That we have allowed the philosophies and vain deceits of Greece and Rome to influence our belief systems.

- That we have built the foundation of our beliefs on the tradition of the Church Fathers rather than on your Word.
- That we have based the doctrines and practices of the church on the traditions and cultures of the world, and not on Christ Jesus our Lord.
- That the restrictions on learning to read kept people from learning the truth.
- That as true faith and morality gradually declined in church leadership, the power to heal gradually declined as well, which led to the belief that normal persons who operated in the power to heal were accused of operating by the power of the devil.

Reformers and Reformation:
I repent for and renounce:

- That as the reformers searched for authority, they became more opposed to the supernatural.
- Their extreme concern for maintaining control, believing that this control was necessary in order to stay alive, consequently stifling the Holy Spirit's moving, speaking, or leading.
- For the Protestant's rejection, envy, and judgment of the miracles occurring in the Catholic Churches before, during, and after the Reformation, even accusing the Catholics of doing miracles by the Devil's power.
- For the Protestant Movement's unbelief and suspicion of the miraculous.

- Wherever the Reformers encouraged legalism, rather than heeding the Spirit of God, to interpret scripture.
- That they did not understand that God's power flows through relationship with God, not through doctrine.

Age of Enlightenment:
I repent for and renounce:

- For the changes in belief, doctrine, and practice made during the age of Enlightenment /Reason, which were based on our human desire to be God.
- For the gradual change in the core of Protestantism from the Word of God to a human authority based in perception and reason. We exalted our minds and devalued His Word.
- For the exaltation of scientific investigation, rather than the Logos and Rhema of the Living God which caused people to explain away miracles as part of the natural order. We repent for redefining miracles into explainable ordinary events.
- That the seminaries taught the pastors not to believe in miracles.
- For allowing skepticism and rationalism to train us that the laws of nature are unbreakable, even by the creator of the universe.
- For rationalism's influence that revelation is not necessary in Christianity.
- For skepticism encouraging doubt in the church.
- For Dispensationalism
- For teaching that the miraculous ended with the death of the Twelve Apostles.

- For the suspicion and fear of emotion, enthusiasm, and experience that entered the Protestant Church during the 1700's.

- For the book by Conyers Middleton, and his refusal to believe in the miraculous no matter what.

- For Thomas Reid's desire to build a foundation of human philosophy instead of the true foundation which is Jesus Christ.

- For the Protestant Church in the USA for establishing Scottish Common-Sense Philosophy in our churches and seminaries. In so doing we put ourselves and our minds in the place of God.

- Every way that the church accepted these attitudes, these philosophies, and put faith in human reason.

- Every way the church believed that by education, humanity could be changed for the better, rather than by the Word and Spirit of God.

- For the liberal, humanist, and modern secularist philosophies which crept into the church due to this belief in education and that relying on the Holy Spirit was not important.

- Regarding Benjamin B. Warfield, we ask forgiveness for: His highly influential and prominent book Counterfeit Miracles, taught in US seminaries, which teaches, contrary to scripture, that the only purpose for miracles is to accredit the gospel, therefore all other miracles are counterfeit. 2. His denial that Spiritual Gifts and Miracles ARE the Gospel of the Kingdom. 3. That most US pastors were trained by his teachings. 4. Continuing Calvin's teaching that Christians cannot have demons. 5. For his statement, "There is no true religion in the world... which is not Calvinistic."

Present Day:
I repent for and renounce:

- All present-day Bible commentaries, handbooks, and teachings which state, agree with, or confirm the belief that miracles have ceased and are no longer available to us.

- All present-day Bible commentaries, handbooks, and teachings which treat the miraculous or prophetic with suspicion, accusation, or devaluation.

- For the intense, ongoing verbal and written criticism of Spirit filled believers by Cessationist believers, and for the effect this verbal strife has had on the Body of Christ alive today.

- For every believer who did not know they were being taught lies when they were being taught Cessationism. Forgive us for not searching scripture for ourselves. Forgive us for passively accepting Cessationist teachings as truth.

- We Declare that:

- Jesus Christ is the only true foundation for the church, her beliefs and practices, and her life.

- In Him dwells all the fullness of the Godhead bodily, and we are complete in Him, who is the Head of all principality and power.

- Jesus Christ is the same yesterday, today, and forever.

- We declare that He has not stopped working miracles on behalf of his people.

- We declare that the Kingdom of God is not of words, but of power!

- We declare that every need we have has been provided by Jesus' death and Resurrection, and this includes healing, deliverance, salvation, provision, protection, guidance, Sonship, and relationship with God the Father.
- We declare that By His Stripes we are healed of every infirmity and weakness.
- We declare that He created us to walk in the fullness of all that He is.
- We declare that He will not withhold any good thing from us, and that we sit in heavenly places in Christ Jesus.
- We declare that His Spirit lives in us, who believe in Jesus Christ the Savior, and this Spirit pours life and health into our beings.
- We declare that Jesus was sent to destroy the works of the Devil, including sickness, sin, poverty, and death.
- We declare that Jesus Christ is the only Light, Truth, and Life, in Him are we fully and abundantly equipped, functioning, and made whole.
- We declare that God will move in our lives, and we will keep our confidence in Him.

14) **Poor Body Care**

The apostles returned to Jesus and told him all that they had done and taught. And he said to them, "Come away by yourselves to a desolate place and rest a while." For many were coming and going, and they had no leisure even to eat. And they went away in the boat to a desolate place by themselves. Mark 6:30-32 (ESV)

God has designed us to function optimally with the appropriate amount of sleep. Our bodies need physical exercise and a healthy diet. Consuming too much sugar, sodium and red meat will eventually lead to physical issues such as cancer, heart disease and diabetes. When we neglect our bodies, we limit our life span. We must do our part!

15) Intense Self-hatred

"Judge not, that you be not judged. For with the judgment you pronounce you will be judged, and with the measure you use it will be measured to you. Why do you see the speck that is in your brother's eye, but do not notice the log that is in your own eye?" Matthew 7:1-3 (ESV)

Bless the Lord, O my soul, and forget not all his benefits, who forgives all your iniquity, who heals all your diseases, who redeems your life from the pit, who crowns you with steadfast love and mercy, who satisfies you with good so that your youth is renewed like the eagle's. Psalm 103:2-5 (ESV)

When we hate, despise or reject ourselves we damage our own immune system. Emotions such as self-rejection may result with a wide spectrum of auto-immune disorders. To break free from an auto-immune disorder like migraine headaches or Hashimoto's disease, we need to ask the Lord to forgive us for rejecting ourselves and renounce the negative declarations we have been speaking against ourselves.

Referred by Paul Cox, a man called me asking for prayer for the debilitating migraines he was having. Immediately I asked him if he dealt with self-hatred (inner conflict). He responded that he did not. "Oh well," I thought, "I missed it!" I then prayed a general prayer of healing and said goodbye.

A day later the man called again and shared that he had walked down the hallway of his home and stopped to look at himself in full length mirror on the wall. He then thought, "I look exactly like my father. I hate my dad so I must hate myself." Abused by his dad in his childhood this man dealt with self-hatred and self-rejection. Aha, I thought and had him pray a prayer like the one below:

A Prayer to Renounce Self-Hatred

I repent and renounce all self-loathing, self-hatred, self-rejection, guilt, condemnation and shame. Father, I thank You for Your forgiveness. Your word says there is therefore now no condemnation for me because I am in Christ Jesus. I break all ties with the spirits of self-hatred, self-rejection, guilt, condemnation and shame, and command them to leave me now. Lift off of me Lord, all shame and self-condemnation in Jesus 'name. Amen.

To the best of my knowledge, this man is no longer dealing with migraine headaches. Thank You Lord Jesus!

16) **Severe Trauma**

When Reuben returned to the pit and saw that Joseph was not in the pit, he tore his clothes and returned to his brothers and said, "The boy is gone, and I, where shall I go?" Then they took Joseph's robe and slaughtered a goat and dipped the robe in the blood. And they sent the robe of many colors and brought it to their father and said, "This we have found; please identify whether it is your son's robe or not." Then Jacob tore his garments and put sackcloth on his loins and mourned for his son many days. And he identified it and said, "It is my son's robe. A fierce animal has devoured him. Joseph is without doubt torn to pieces." All his sons and all his daughters rose up to comfort him, but he refused to be comforted and said, "No, I shall go down to Sheol to my son, mourning." Thus his father wept for him. Meanwhile the Midianites had sold him in Egypt to Potiphar, an officer of Pharaoh, the captain of the guard. Genesis 37: 29-37 (ESV)

2 Samuel 13:1 (ESV)

When a person has been traumatized, <u>Post Traumatic Stress Syndrome</u> (PTSD) can set in between 1 to 3 months later. If not dealt with via prayer, ongoing counseling and sustained social support a person's cells can be negatively impacted at a cellular and sub-cellular level resulting in wide spectrum of physical issues such as:

- Anxiety
- Strokes
- Depression
- Headaches
- Sleep issues
- Muscle tension
- Digestive issues
- Reproductive issues
- High blood pressure

- Problems with memory and focus

According to Harvard Health: "Exposure to ongoing stressors can keep cortisol levels consistently high, which can wear down the body on a cellular level, according to the research team. They added that other studies have suggested this reaction may raise the risk of cancer or cause existing cancer to spread more rapidly."

Studies have shown that when the stress hormone cortisol is secreted into a person's bloodstream, as the result of a traumatic experience, their glucose levels rise dramatically affecting both their immune and reproductive systems.

A Prayer to Abolish Fear

Father, I come as your child, your heir, to repent on behalf of my generational line and myself for all of us who have failed to recognize our position and authority in Christ Jesus, choosing to be intimidated by fear rather than trusting you to be sufficient for all of our needs. Please forgive us for all of the times that we have set our eyes on the cares of the world instead of seeking You first.

I repent for any instance in which we have frightened others through words or actions, becoming fear mongers who spread false teachings and the deceitfulness of the world. I now declare the truth that You, Lord, are my light and my salvation; of whom shall I be afraid? You are the strength of my life so whom should I fear? You are my hiding place, my deliverer and protector, and I choose now to take up the full armor of God and use all of the weapons you put at my disposal to resist fear, knowing that it must flee in the face of faith.

In times when I am tempted to be afraid, I now choose to be strong and to let my heart take courage as I wait for You. I choose to change my thinking and set my mind on things above, looking to You as my deliverer, for I am persuaded that nothing in any physical or spiritual dimension is able to separate me from Your love.

Father, Lord Jesus, Holy Spirit; You are my perfect love and I trust You now to cast fear out of my life according to your promise, and I ask for a seven-fold return through the blood of Jesus of all that the enemy has stolen from me through fear and all of its by-products; I ask for your joy to well up within me and bubble over onto everyone I encounter; I boldly ask for the gift of faith to live with the assurance of things hoped for and the conviction of things not seen, faith to move the mountains in my life and to live in victory through Christ Jesus.

I declare that this is the foundation of my faith; God is real, His Word is true; Jesus said it so I believe it, and I must always seek Him first. My life is His; He is my refuge and strength, my place of rest, my peace and my hope; He meets my every need. With Him on my side, I willingly choose to join the battle!

17) Sexual Immorality and Victimization

Do you not know that your bodies are members of Christ? Shall I then take the members of Christ and make them members of a prostitute? Never! Or do you not know that he who is joined to a prostitute becomes one body with her? For, as it is written, "The two will become one flesh." But he who is joined to the Lord becomes one spirit with him. Flee from sexual immorality. Every other sin a person commits is outside the body, but the sexually immoral person sins against his own body. Or do you not know that your body is a temple of the Holy Spirit within you, whom you have from God? You are not your own, for you were bought with a price. So glorify God in your body. 1 Corinthians 6:15-20 (ESV)

According to the above passage when we sin sexually, we hurt ourselves physically, and it's clear in 2 Samuel 13:1-20 that when we have been sexually victimized our emotions can be severely affected. David's daughter, Tamar, had been raped by her half-brother Amnon and as a result, she was physically, emotionally and spiritually devastated! Feeling defiled and ashamed because she had lost her virginity in such a cruel way she lived in isolation in her brother's house.

Entrapment in Sheol:
A decade ago, a female attorney approached my wife and I for a ministry appointment. When we met, she shared that she had been raped by a client of her firm in-spite of pleading with him not to do it. After raping her he threatened to remove his business from the firm if she told her partners what he had done to her. Unable to function she locked herself in her office for weeks and fell behind on her work. After one of her firm's partners approached her, she shared what happened and sought our help.

This woman was unable to function at her job because of the trauma she had experienced when she was raped. When a person is traumatized, they are riddled with fear and anxiety. The Greek word for anxiety is *merimna,* meaning to be split in different directions. When an individual is traumatized parts of his or her soul are scattered into pieces and become entrapped in the ungodly depth otherwise known in Scripture as Sheol. An example of this kind of spiritual entrapment can be found in Psalm 88:3-6 (ESV):

> *For my soul is full of troubles, and my life draws near to Sheol. I am counted among those who go down to the pit; I am a man who has no strength, like one set loose among the dead, like the slain that lie in the grave, like those whom you remember no more, for they are cut off from your hand. You have put me in the depths of the pit, in the regions dark and deep.*

Are Scattered Parts Mentioned in the Bible as the Result of Trauma?

The below verses confirm that traumatic incidents can indeed scatter our spirit and soul parts into pieces:

> *2 Chronicles 15:4-6 (ESV):* **They were broken in pieces. Nation was crushed by nation and city by city, for God troubled them with every sort of distress. In those times there was no peace to him who went out or to him who came in, for great disturbances afflicted all the inhabitants of the lands. For a long time Israel was without the true God, and without a teaching priest and without law, but when in their distress they turned to the Lord, the God of Israel, and sought him, he was found by them.**

> *Job 17:1 (ESV):* **My spirit is broken; my days are extinct; the graveyard is ready for me.**

> *Psalm 7:1-2 (ESV):* **O Lord my God, in you do I take refuge; save me from all my pursuers and deliver me, lest like a lion they tear my soul apart, rending it in pieces, with none to deliver.**

*Psalm 34:18 (ESV): **The Lord is near to the brokenhearted and saves the crushed in spirit.***

*Psalm 69:20 (ESV): **Reproaches have broken my heart, so that I am in despair. I looked for pity, but there was none, and for comforters, but I found none.***

The Book of Proverbs explains the spiritual reality of both entrapment in Sheol and also harassment by the spirits of the departed:

So you will be delivered from the forbidden woman, from the adulteress with her smooth words, who forsakes the companion of her youth and forgets the covenant of her God; for her house sinks down to death, and her paths to the departed; none who go to her come back, nor do they regain the paths of life. Proverbs 2:16-18 (ESV)

The woman Folly is loud; she is seductive and knows nothing. She sits at the door of her house; she takes a seat on the highest places of the town, calling to those who pass by, who are going straight on their way, "Whoever is simple, let him turn in here!" And to him who lacks sense she says, "Stolen water is sweet, and bread eaten in secret is pleasant." But he does not know that the dead are there, that her guests are in the depths of Sheol. Proverbs 9:13-18 (ESV)

These two passages remind us about the spiritual consequences of venturing sexually outside of the marriage bed. Whether victimization (rape or molestation), an act of infidelity or paying a prostitute for a one night stand these ungodly sexual liasons entrap the soul (mind, will, emotions) in the depths of Sheol causing individuals to become oppressed by the 'departed.' The Hebrew word for 'departed' is *repayim*, from which the word *rephaim* is derived; *Rephaim* is translated 'giants' in some Old Testament passages, but is also rendered as 'the spirits of the departed'; 'the dead ones' or 'shades.' (See Rephaim/Jewishvirtuallibrary.org)

Sexual sin and acts such a rape, incest and molestation give the enemy the legal right to keep people chained to the realm of darkness and blocks God's healing power from setting them free from infirmity. When we are unfaithful to our spouse or sleep with a prostitute we become spiritually tied to the Underworld. I realize that this seems like a page out of a science fiction novel, but according to the Bible, this is what transpires in the spiritual realm.

To wrap up, my wife and I prayed the attorney out of Sheol and as far as I know she is now married and thriving. God is better than good!

A Prayer to Break Free from the Consequences of Sexual Immorality

Lord Jesus, I confess here and now that you are my Creator (John 1:3) and therefore the creator of my sexuality. I confess that you are also my Savior, that you have ransomed me with your blood (1 Corinthians 15:3, Matthew 20:28). I have been bought with the blood of Jesus Christ; my life and my body belong to you (1 Corinthians 6:19–20). Lord, I present myself to you now to be made whole and holy in every way including in my sexuality. You ask us to present our bodies to you as living sacrifices (Romans 12:1) and the parts of our bodies as instruments of righteousness (Romans 6:13). I do this now. I present my body, my sexuality [specify gender] as a man/ woman, and I present my sexual nature to you. I consecrate my sexuality to you.

Jesus, I ask your Holy Spirit to help me now remember, confess, and renounce my sexual sins. [Pause. Listen. Remember. Confess and renounce.] Lord Jesus, I ask your forgiveness for every act of sexual sin. You promised that if I confess my sins, you are faithful and just to forgive me of my sins and cleanse me from all unrighteousness (1 John 1:9). I ask you now to cleanse me of my sexual sins; cleanse my body, my soul, and my spirit, cleanse my heart and mind and will, cleanse my sexuality. Thank you for forgiving me and cleansing me. I receive your forgiveness and cleansing. I renounce every claim I have given Satan to my life or sexuality through my sexual sins. Those claims are now broken by the cross and blood of Jesus Christ (Colossians 2:13–15). Lord Jesus, I thank you for offering me total and complete forgiveness. I receive that forgiveness now. I choose to forgive myself for all of my sexual wrongdoing. I also choose to forgive those who have harmed me sexually. [Be specific here; name those people and forgive them.] I release them to you, Jesus. I release all my anger and judgment toward them. The Cross is enough. Come, Lord Jesus, into the pain they caused me, and heal me with your love.

I now bring the cross of my Lord Jesus Christ between me and every person with whom I have been sexually intimate outside of marriage. [Name them specifically whenever possible. Also name those who have abused you sexually.] I break all sexual, emotional, and spiritual bonds with [name the person if possible, or just "that girl in high school" if you can't remember her name]. I keep the cross of Christ between us.

Lord Jesus, I now consecrate my sexuality to you in every way. I consecrate my sexual intimacy with my spouse to you. I ask you to cleanse and heal my sexuality and our marital sexual intimacy in every way. I ask your healing grace to come and free me from all consequences of sexual sin. I ask you to fill my sexuality with your healing love and goodness. Restore my sexuality in wholeness. Let my spouse and me experience all of the intimacy and pleasure you intended a man and woman to enjoy in marriage. I invite the Spirit of God to fill our marriage bed now. Or, [if you're single] until that day that I get to be married, I continue to consecrate my sexuality to Jesus Christ. I pray all of this in the name of Jesus Christ, my Lord. Amen!

18. Bronze Doors

Thus says the Lord to his anointed, to Cyrus, whose right hand I have grasped, to subdue nations before him and to loose the belts of kings, to open doors before him that gates may not be closed: "I will go before you and level the exalted places, I will break in pieces the doors of bronze and cut through the bars of iron... Isaiah 45:1-2 (ESV)

Over a decade ago one of the elders of our church informed me that he had gone to the doctor because of a lung issue he was having. He had an MRI and was told by his doctor over the phone that he needed to schedule a second appointment asap because a dark ominous spot showed up on his scan.

Prior to learning about this man's dire condition, Paul Cox shared with me how bronze gates and iron doors, in the spirit realm, can keep people imprisoned in physical bondage. In Scripture the color bronze symbolizes God's righteous judgment. According to the book of Jeremiah the Lord exiled His people to the land of Babylon where they were held captive against their will (in bronze doors and iron gates) because they had persistently rebelled against Him. We can reasonably conclude then that bronze gates and iron bars can indeed symbolize physical captivity or disease.

So, what happened to the man with the bad lung? I placed my hand over his chest and discerned the presence of a bronze door. I then asked the Lord to open the bronze door so that the righteous gate behind it could be opened and asked the King of Glory (Psalm 24) to come in and heal his lungs.

The next day the man, who had been told by his doctor that there was an ominous spot on his lungs, called and told me that a second scan revealed that the spot or mass or whatever it was, was gone!

Summary:
The above list that I have mentioned in this chapter is not exhaustive. My hope and prayer has been to help you understand how divine healing can be hindered and how to remove those hindrances so that the Holy Spirit can heal you.

In the next chapter I will unpack our role in the healing process.

[1] https://singjupost.com/derek-prince-invisible-barriers-to-healing-full-transcript/

[2] Ibid.

Chapter Eight
Taking Responsibility for Your Healing
Rob Gross

It has been my observation, over the last three decades of praying for the sick, that many people want God to heal them without doing their part. By doing their part I mean obeying God's Word, being mindful of their declarations, changing their diets, letting go of their offenses, renouncing debilitating lies, getting more sleep and drinking more water to name just a few. Deuteronomy 29:29 (ESV) says:

> *The secret things belong to the LORD our God, but the things that are revealed belong to us and to our children forever, that we may do all the words of this law.*

Psalm 19:7-11 (ESV) also encourages us that 'when' and 'if' we sync our lives with His words we reap the benefits.

> *The law of the Lord is perfect, <u>reviving the soul</u>; the testimony of the Lord is sure, making wise the simple; the precepts of the Lord are right, <u>rejoicing the heart</u>; the commandment of the Lord is pure, <u>enlightening the eyes</u>; the fear of the Lord is clean, enduring forever; the rules of the Lord are true, and righteous altogether. More to be desired are they than gold, even much fine gold; sweeter also than honey and drippings of the honeycomb. Moreover, by them is your servant warned; <u>in keeping them there is great reward.</u>*

God has done His part, so we are able to access His healing power (Isaiah 53:5) but according to the passages cited above we must do our part as well. What does this look like?

In his book, *A More Excellent Way*, Henry Wright identified "8 Rs to Freedom":

- Recognize
- Responsibility
- Repent
- Renounce
- Remove
- Resist
- Rejoice
- Restore

Using those 'R's', let me suggest what each of these might look like as we implement them in our lives.

Recognize:
Recognizing the root of any issue whether physical, emotional or spiritual requires both honest reflection and in some cases spiritual discernment (Hebrews 5:14). Of all the steps tracing the fruit to the root is the most challenging in the healing process. Once the root domino is identified the other dominos will fall.

Responsibility:
Taking personal responsibility for your actions and attitudes is a major step in the healing process that requires humility. 1 Peter 5:5 says that God gives grace to the humble but is opposed to the proud or self-sufficient. God's undeserved healing favor flows to those who willingly acknowledge their sins (1 John 5:5).

Repent:
To repent means to change your attitude. It means to turn around 180 degrees and go the opposite direction. When we wholeheartedly repent the Lord's refreshing, transforming love will begin to wash over us.

Renounce:
To renounce a debilitating habit or attitude literally means, "To break ties with the enemy." Genuine repentance always leads to breaking unhealthy ties with the prince of darkness and his realm. This process is called renunciation.

Remove:
If you are willingly engaged in sinful behavior don't expect the Lord to heal you unless you're willing to remove the demonic plaque clogging the arteries of your heart. To put it another way if you get rid of the garbage (bitterness, hatred, offense), you will get rid of the rats.

Resist:
Resistance against the schemes of darkness starts with being submitted to the Lordship of Jesus Christ. This raises the obvious question is Jesus 100% the Lord of your life? King Saul had no heart for God, King Solomon had half a heart for God. Both kings walked away from the Lord and did not finish well. But because King David had a whole heart for God, he fulfilled God's purpose for his life. When we give God 100% the devil will leave, but if we give only 50% or 0%, he will swoop down like a vulture and feast on our carcass.

Rejoice:
It's a choice to rejoice. The joy of the Lord is your strength. Choose to rejoice at all times and the Lord will strengthen you through the darkest of times.

Restore:
One of the wisest steps you can take when facing a life-threatening disease is to pray for others who are facing a similar situation. A powerful spiritual transaction takes place when we take the time to love and pray for someone who is suffering. By choosing to bless and restore others God will restore and bless you.

CHAPTER NINE:
WHERE DO WE GO FROM HERE?

ROB GROSS

Now the eleven disciples went to Galilee, to the mountain to which Jesus had directed them. And when they saw him they worshiped him, but some doubted. And Jesus came and said to them, "All authority in heaven and on earth has been given to me. Go therefore and make disciples of all nations, baptizing them in the name of the Father and of the Son and of the Holy Spirit, teaching them to observe all that I have commanded you. And behold, I am with you always, to the end of the age." Matthew 28:16-20 (ESV)

So when they had come together, they asked him, "Lord, will you at this time restore the kingdom to Israel?" He said to them, "It is not for you to know times or seasons that the Father has fixed by his own authority. But you will receive power when the Holy Spirit has come upon you, and you will be my witnesses in Jerusalem and in all Judea and Samaria, and to the end of the earth." Acts 1:8 (ESV)

The Great Commission:
When Jesus commissioned His spiritual sons and daughters to take the Gospel to every nation He did, in my opinion, a remarkable thing. What did He do? I'm glad you asked. When Jesus commissioned His band of 120 believers to take the Gospel into all the world, He entrusted His plan to reach people of every generation solely in their hands (and our

162

hands). I don't know about you, but I find this mind blowing! I find it mind blowing because all of us are imperfect byproducts of the Fall. Filled with fear and shame we often feel weak, inadequate and totally unqualified to be vessels through whom God moves to reach broken people who aren't seeking Him.

Acts 1:8 reminds us that we need the power of the Holy Spirit to reach people for Christ. It reminds us that without God's power we cannot reach the hearts of those who are bound in darkness by a supernatural enemy. Jesus made this explicitly clear in Luke 4:18-19 (ESV):

> *The Spirit of the Lord is upon me, because he has anointed me to proclaim good news to the poor. He has sent me to proclaim liberty to the captives and recovering of sight to the blind, to set at liberty those who are oppressed, to proclaim the year of the Lord's favor.*

God is Waiting on Us:
In 2018, I had a dream where I was with my mother on Waikiki beach on the southern shore of Oahu. As I looked towards the horizon I saw an enormous wave hurtling towards us. I turned to my 92-year-old mom and said, "Mom, turn around and walk as quickly as you can. We need to get to higher ground!"

Well, as you might imagine my elderly mom did not sprint off of the beach. Looking back with concern I saw the wave building in height as it got closer to the shoreline until it was literally above us. This part of the dream was so real that I could feel drops of water brushing against my face. At this moment I thought, "We're gonna die!" Then suddenly an enormous hand came out of nowhere and held back the wave. My mom and I then got off the beach and got to higher ground and the dream ended.

As I pondered the meaning of this dream, I recognized that my slow moving mother represented the church of Hawaii that was not prepared for the enormous wave of revival that was headed our way. And then the Lord whispered to my spirit and said, "The church is not waiting on Me to send revival, I am waiting on the church to prepare for revival."

Preparation is Crucial:
We are not waiting on God; God is waiting on us! His desire is to pour out His Spirit upon us, but the present-day pastor-teacher structure of the church will not be able to hold the enormous harvest that He intends to send. This is why the Lord is presently raising up apostles, prophets and evangelists to prepare the church for what is coming.

What Does God's Governmental Structure Look Like?
And He Himself gave some to be apostles, some prophets, some evangelists, and some pastors and teachers, for the equipping of the saints for the work of ministry, for the edifying of the body of Christ, till we all come to the unity of the faith and of the knowledge of the Son of God, to a perfect man, to the measure of the stature of the fullness of Christ; but, speaking the truth in love, may grow up in all things into Him who is the head—Christ—that we should no longer be children, tossed to and fro and carried about with every wind of doctrine, by the trickery of men, in the cunning craftiness of deceitful plotting, from whom the whole body, joined and knit together by what every joint supplies, according to the effective working by which every part does its share, causes growth of

the body for the edifying of itself in love. Ephesians
4:11-16 (NKJV)

Note the word 'till' (or 'until' as rendered in other translations) in verse 13. The five offices of Jesus are needed 'till' or 'until' the Body of Christ comes into unity fulfilling the Lord's prayer in John 17. The five offices of Jesus are needed 'till' or 'until' the family of God knows the Lord on an intimate basis. Jesus longs for a pure and spotless Bride that is passionately in love with Him. The five offices of Jesus are needed 'till' or 'until' the *ekklesia* is mature in the stature of Christ meaning that it will be able to exercise its' powers of discernment to distinguish between good and evil (Hebrews 5:14).

So, here's several 20-million-dollar questions to consider: 1) Are Catholics and Protestants in complete unity with one another? 2) Are those of us who are Pentecostals and Charismatics in unity with conservative Evangelicals? 3) Are we passionately in love with Jesus to the point where we are willing to obey His commands in-spite of the cost? 4) Are we raising up weekend attenders or mature kingdom-warriors who are walking in Sonship thus fulfilling Romans 8:19?

As I survey the spiritual landscape of the church today it is in greater unity than ever before, but we can still grow in this area. I have observed that there are more passionate, Spirit-filled believers popping up everywhere. However, there are still many believers who are spiritually asleep or not actively a part of the Body because of the Pandemic and other reasons. As far as growing into the stature of Christ the Body has also advanced as more believers are learning how to heal the sick and cast out demons. The caterpillar is slowly transitioning out of its' cocoon, but still has a way to go before becoming the butterfly the Lord wants it to become.

As mentioned previously in Chapter Four, we need to embrace God's fivefold structure of church government if we want to function as mature sons and daughters who know what their Father is doing. With this in mind, I'd like to further explore what each of the fivefold officers of Christ bring to the table and why they are needed today for us to advance the kingdom of God into the future.

Apostles Build:
> *According to the grace of God given to me, like a skilled master builder I laid a foundation, and someone else is building upon it. Let each one take care how he builds upon it.* 1 *Corinthians 3:10 (ESV)*

Apostles build upon the cornerstone of Christ by laying a foundation for the gospel of the kingdom to advance. Mentioned 80 times in the New Testament, apostles build systems that establish kingdom culture in the church. This culture includes, but is not limited to:

- Fathering and mothering the Body of Christ into mature sons and daughters.
- Raising up healthy, passionate sons and daughters who wholeheartedly love God and desire to advance the Father's agenda in the earth.
- Establishing a supernatural culture of the miraculous that is the norm instead of the exception.
- Planting freedom outposts that set the captives free from physical and spiritual bondages.

- Identifying, calling forth and commissioning emerging five fold officers and setting them in place in the Body of Christ.
- Healing, deliverance and the gifts of the Holy Spirit.
- Trailblazing, pioneering and introducing new insights from heaven that enable families to heal and grow in Christlike character.

Prophets Reveal:
For the Lord God does nothing without revealing his secret to his servants the prophets. Amos 3:7 (ESV)

Mentioned 172 x's in Scripture prophets not only reveal the Father's agenda (Acts 21:10), but they also train the Body of Christ to hear the Father's voice for themselves so they can comfort, encourage and build up the Body of Christ. God's people need to know, from time to time, that they are loved and appreciated by the Lord. They also need ongoing encouragement to keep persevering in the face of enemy opposition and the trials of life. True office prophets not only reveal what the Lord is saying, they teach others to do the same.

Evangelists Gather:
And when we had finished our voyage from Tyre, we came to Ptolemais, greeted the brethren, and stayed with them one day. On the next day we who were Paul's companions departed and came to Caesarea, and entered the house of Philip the evangelist, who was one of the seven, and stayed with him. Acts 21:7-8 (NKJV)

New Testament evangelists like Greg Laurie are anointed by God to gather the Lost in significant numbers and win them to Jesus. The call of an evangelist, however, is to do more than lead thousands to Jesus in large meetings. The call of an evangelist is also to train the Body of Christ to share the Gospel themselves thus expanding the Gospel's reach and effectiveness.

Pastors Care:
And He Himself gave some to be apostles, some prophets, some evangelists, and some pastors and teachers... Ephesians 4:11 (NKJV)

A closer look at Scripture reveals that the term 'pastor' (singular tense) is not found in the Bible. The term 'pastors' (plural tense) is used, but only once. It seems, upon closer examination, that elders or overseers shepherded God's flock in the First Century not pastors. 1 Timothy 3:1-7 (ESV) provides a job description of the office of overseer:

The saying is trustworthy: If anyone aspires to the office of overseer, he desires a noble task. Therefore an overseer must be above reproach, the husband of one wife, sober-minded, self-controlled, respectable, hospitable, able to teach, not a drunkard, not violent but gentle, not quarrelsome, not a lover of money. He must manage his own household well, with all dignity keeping his children submissive, for if someone does not know how to manage his own household, how will he care for God's church? He must not be a recent convert, or he may become puffed up with conceit and fall into the condemnation of the devil. Moreover, he must be well thought of by outsiders, so that he may not fall into disgrace, into a snare of the devil.

The absence of pastors in the New Testament is a head scratcher. In-spite of this the office of pastor is the primary leadership role and title in the present-day church. We have senior pastors, associate pastors, assistant pastors and youth pastors. Every leader is called a pastor.

I have been a pastor for over thirty years so don't miss my heart. God loves pastors and so do I! But something is off because we have been reproducing pew sitters instead of kingdom warriors. Something is amiss and it's obvious that it's because the other four offices have not been afforded the same weight as the office of pastor.

In-spite of tremendous opposition and ongoing persecution, the Acts church penetrated every facet of Roman society including Caesar's household. If we are going to impact our society like the early church, we must allow the Holy Spirit to restore and re-establish the five offices of Jesus in our midst.

Teachers Explain:
> *Now there were in the church at Antioch prophets and teachers, Barnabas, Simeon who was called Niger, Lucius of Cyrene, Manaen a lifelong friend of Herod the tetrarch, and Saul.* Acts 13:1 (ESV)

Mentioned 13 x's in Scripture the office of teacher is prominent in the church today. Chuck Swindoll and Joyce Myers, for example, have helped tens of thousands of believers understand and apply the Bible to their everyday lives.

Without understanding God's blueprint for living the Body of Christ will sail off into heresy and error. More than ever, we need to pray for the Lord to raise up more office teachers not only to teach the Bible, but to teach believers how to study the Bible for themselves.

In sum, if we get in-sync with God's governmental order, the kingdom of heaven (Matthew 6:9-10) will come and we will transition from being spectators in the stands to kingdom players on the field.

In Chapter Ten I will draw this book to a close by encouraging you to step out by faith and believe that God is still performing miracles today.

CHAPTER TEN:
BELIEVING GOD FOR THE GREATER THINGS
ROB GROSS

Truly, truly, I say to you, whoever believes in me will also do the works that I do; and greater works than these will he do, because I am going to the Father. Philip said to him, "Lord, show us the Father, and it is enough for us." Jesus said to him, "Have I been with you so long, and you still do not know me, Philip? Whoever has seen me has seen the Father. How can you say, 'Show us the Father'? Do you not believe that I am in the Father and the Father is in me? The words that I say to you I do not speak on my own authority, but the Father who dwells in me does his works. Believe me that I am in the Father and the Father is in me, or else believe on account of the works themselves. Whatever you ask in my name, this I will do, that the Father may be glorified in the Son. If you ask me anything in my name, I will do it." John 14:8-14 (ESV)

Do We Believe What God Has Said?
On December 27th, 2016, Larry Pearson sent me the following prophetic word:

> Ok dude last night I had a dream that had you in it. I saw you in a gathering and it felt like I was present in real time. The gathering had probably 4-5 thousand people. Testimonials of major miracles and wonders were the focus. Then I also saw some of your people. There were unusual supernatural

activities happening with them out on a major highway like the highway here in Ontario. Ontario means, 'Beautiful Water'. I'm not sure what this means, but I'd say you're coming into a huge wave of the miracle working I AM.

Jesus the Miracle Worker:
Jesus Christ is the same yesterday and today and forever. Hebrews 13:8 (ESV)

Jesus did extraordinary miracles yesterday, today and forever, which means, according to Hebrews 13:8, that He is still doing miracles today through us. The name Christ means, 'the Anointed One.' The name Christian means, 'little Christ' implying that we are anointed or divinely empowered by the Holy Spirit not only to do the same works of Jesus, but to perform even greater works than Jesus.

The challenge that many believers struggle with today is they do not believe what the Bible says. In John 14:12 Jesus declared that those who followed Him would do greater works than He had done. If Jesus said it, it must be true! I have personally witnessed over 50 confirmed miracles in the last 30 years. Because I have already shared several of these miraculous stories throughout this book, I have only listed 8 other testimonies to encourage you to believe that John 14:12 is true beyond doubt.

A Mother with Multiple Tumors Healed in Jesus Name!
After receiving an impartation to heal the sick at the end of a Sunday service a woman went home to pray for her mother who had multiple cancerous lumps in both of her breasts. The next day the mom went to see her oncologist for a previously scheduled appointment. While waiting to see her doctor she exclaimed to the nurses, "God healed

me!" Soon after she asked for a scan insisting again that the Lord had healed her. They tested her and all the lumps in both breasts had miraculously disappeared! The Bible says in Psalm 23:6 that goodness and mercy doggedly pursue us all the days of our lives.

A Woman Delivered from the Spirit of Infirmity!

On any given Sunday morning our prayer team does most of the praying for the sick. Most of the time I simply walk around and see if anyone needs assistance. On one occasion I walked by a woman receiving prayer who was in a considerable amount of back pain. All of a sudden, I had this thought, "Tell the spirits of pain and infirmity to leave." As soon as I uttered these words in Jesus Name, the woman crumpled to the floor. Needing to attend to other matters I left the scene not knowing what the Lord had done. Two days later I received an email from this woman saying that God had healed her back. Like the woman with a disabling spirit in Luke 13:10-13, Jesus set her free!

A Woman Healed of Sleep Deprivation!

At a Sunday afternoon training class, where multiple church members from the Body of Christ attended, the Lord healed a woman of a hiatal hernia (A hiatal hernia happens when the upper part of the stomach bulges through the large muscle that separates the abdomen and the chest and can sometime lead to heartburn and abdominal pain). [mayoclinic.org] Her condition was so severe that she had not slept well for years. After praying for her, she said that she felt something shift inside of her and knew that God had healed her. Seven years later I bumped into her at a youth camp, and she reported that she was still free of this debilitating condition. God is better than good!

A Sign and a Wonder!

In 1998, a retired woman asked for prayer for her ailing lower back. To my amazement, after mumbling a quick prayer, the Holy Spirit bent her so far backwards that her head almost touched the floor. As I was watching the Lord do this, the first thought that came into my head was, "She's doing the limbo" (a dance or contest that involves bending over backwards and passing under a horizontal pole lowered slightly for each successive pass). After twenty long seconds the Holy Spirit lifted her up to a standing position and she reported that her back felt great!

Stage 4 Cancer Healed!
I received an unexpected email from a man that I did not know who had been impacted by the Lord at the conclusion of one of our Sunday services a year earlier and wanted to tell me about it. I obliged him and we met a few days later for lunch. During this time, he shared that he had attended our service with his wife and had come to our service to receive prayer because he had stage 4 cancer.

On the Sunday this man and his wife attended our service we did not pray for the sick. Instead, because of the Holy Spirit's leading we invited people to walk through a healing gate that I had discerned. The man walked through the gate with his wife at the front of the sanctuary and left.

The next day he visited his oncologist's office for a PET scan (A positron emission tomography (PET) scan is a radioactive imaging test that can detect early signs of cancer, heart disease and brain conditions). The results came back and showed no sign of cancer whatsoever!

Prior to saying goodbye, he handed me an envelope with a large check in it made payable to our church. The Lord had saved his life, and he was truly grateful. TYJ!

Multiple Benign Tumors Gone in Jesus Name!
The following testimony was emailed to me from a woman who lives in Florida. In October 2023, she attended our 2nd Annual Apostolic Conference at our church facility on Oahu and was miraculously healed by the Lord:

> After I asked prayer for a suspected pituitary tumor, Justin and I felt there was a very specific path we were to walk. We felt led to ask 9 people to pray, and we were led to pray that the tumor dissolved before my 2nd round of tests, and that nothing could be found. One of the 9 was Kevin Wada. The day before my next round of tests, he prayed for me, commanding the tumor to be dissolved in Jesus' name. I had an immediate response to the prayer and the pain was excruciating, but I knew the Lord had begun dissolving it. My next round of tests finished up on day 40 of the headaches, and although I didn't feel better that day, I was filled with joy. By the time my results came back later that week, the headaches had begun to lift. At my appointment, the endocrinologist was astonished to report that there was suddenly no sign of a tumor, and all previous abnormal levels were now well inside normal. She had no explanation and did not know what to tell me, except that she doesn't know what happened and as long as the headaches continued to lift, she was satisfied there's no further investigation needed. I'm now 2 weeks symptom free and very grateful! Thank you for your prayers for me and my family, we value them greatly. In October the Lord started telling me that I would be a first fruit of Hawaii. I didn't know what He meant by that! Because we asked 9 people to pray, and 9 is

connected to fruit bearing (Galatians 5:22) And because my healing happened during the month of Shevat which is when the Jewish people celebrate the trees ability to bear its first fruit, I am now wondering if what happened to me is a picture of what we are going to begin to experience as the waves of God's power that began in Hawaii begins to pour through the pipeline to the nations.

A Cracked Tooth Healed!

November 27, 2023, I grew up in Nanakuli, HI, and graduated from Nanakuli High School. After graduating, I went to New Hope Christian College in Eugene, OR, where I met the Lord while pursuing a degree in counseling. I have been serving Him faithfully and learning to be His disciple ever since. I just moved back home in September after eight years of being in Oregon and was invited to MVCC by Melodi and Ray Stockton. I do not know what God has for me next, but I know He is FAITHFUL to lead me, especially in times of uncertainty. So, I am trusting Him, and I am excited to see what He does in this new season of my life being back home in Hawaii! I had a tooth that was infected, fractured, and scheduled to be extracted. I had been fervently praying for the Lord's healing in my tooth and gums and I received prayed for it on Sunday, November 26. The Lord completely healed my tooth. I had a follow up appointment today and when they looked at it, they said there was no fracture and no infection and told me that there was no need to extract it. PRAISE THE LORD!

A Pastor Healed of Nose Cancer!

In 2002 a senior pastor and his associate pastor sat across from me at our office. The senior pastor, who I met with for coffee periodically, had brought his associate with him to receive prayer. When I asked the associate what he needed prayer for her said, "Nose cancer." Because he was Chinese I asked him, "Did you or anyone in your family worship Kwan Yin (Kwan Yin is often referred to as the "most widely beloved Buddhist Divinity"with miraculous powers to assist all those who pray to her, as is mentioned in the *Pumen chapter* of the *Lotus Sutra* and the *Kāraṇḍavyūha Sūtra*)?" [Wikipedia, Kwan Yin] He responded yes and I encouraged him to repent for and renounce the worship of this false god on behalf of his family which he gladly did.

Several years later I visited this man's church and met with him. I asked him how was doing and he said that after praying to break ties with Kwan Yin the Lord healed him of nose cancer!

Romans 8:19 says that all of creation is waiting for the people of God to step into their supernatural call to effect transformative change throughout the earth. My prayer, as I conclude this book, is that you will 'dare to believe' God for the greater things and see Him glorified through you! Yes you!

Appendix One:
A Hebrew/Greek Word Study About Healing

Old Testament - Hebrew Words for Healing:

1. *Rapha* (OT:7495) means to mend; cure; heal; repair; make whole. It is translated in the KJV as: cure; make whole; heal; healed; healeth; thoroughly healed; physician.

   Bless the Lord, O my soul; And all that is within me, bless His holy name! Bless the Lord, O my soul, And forget not all His benefits: Who forgives all your iniquities, Who <u>heals</u> all your diseases, Who redeems your life from destruction, Who crowns you with lovingkindness and tender mercies, Who satisfies your mouth with good things, So that your youth is renewed like the eagle's. Psalm 103:1-5 (NKJV)

   But He was wounded for our transgressions, He was bruised for our iniquities; The chastisement for our peace was upon Him, And by His stripes we are <u>healed</u>. Isaiah 53:5 (NKJV)

   Who forgives all your iniquities, Who <u>heals</u> all your diseases. Psalms 103:3 (NKJV)

2. *Marpe* (OT:4832) means curative; a medicine: a cure; deliverance. It is translated in the KJV as: cure; curable; healing; health; remedy; sound; wholesome; yielding.

   For they are life to those who find them, And <u>health</u> to all their flesh. Proverbs 4:22 (NKJV)

178

The following scripture has three different Hebrew words in it that all mean health and cure:

Behold, I will bring it <u>health</u> (aruwkah) and <u>cure</u> (marpe), and I will <u>cure</u> (rapha) them, and will reveal unto them the abundance of peace and truth. Jeremiah 33:6 (KJV)

3. **Yeshuwah** (OT:3444) means something saved; deliverance; aid; victory; prosperity. It is translated in the KJV as: deliverance; health; help; helping; salvation; save; saving (health); welfare.

Why art thou cast down, O my soul? and why art thou disquieted within me? hope thou in God: for I shall yet praise him, who is the <u>health</u> of my countenance, and my God. Psalms 42:11 (KJV)

With long life I will satisfy him And show him My <u>salvation</u>. Psalms 91:16 (NKJV)

4. **Aruwkah** (OT:724) means restoration to sound health; wholeness. It is translated in the KJV as: health; made up; perfected.

Then your light shall break forth like the morning, Your <u>healing</u> shall spring forth speedily, And your righteousness shall go before you; The glory of the Lord shall be your rear guard. Isaiah 58:8 NKJV

5. **Chabash** (OT:2280) means to wrap firmly; to stop; to rule; health. It is translated in the KJV as: bind (up); gird about; govern; healer; put; saddle; wrap about.

The Spirit of the Lord God is upon Me, Because the Lord has anointed Me To preach good tidings to the poor; He has sent Me to <u>heal</u> the brokenhearted, To *proclaim liberty to the captives, And the opening of the prison to those who are bound. Isaiah 61:1 (NKJV)*

He <u>heals</u> the brokenhearted and binds up their wounds. Psalms 147:3 (NKJV)

6. *Riphuth* OT:7500) means a cure; health. It is translated in the KJV as health.

    It will be health to your flesh, And strength to your bones. Proverbs 3:8 (NKJV)

NEW TESTAMENT - GREEK WORDS FOR HEALING:

7. *Therapeuo* (NT:2323) means: to wait upon menially, to adore (God): to relieve (of disease). It is translated in the KJV as: cure; heal; worship.

    Now He could do no mighty work there, except that He laid His hands on a few sick people and healed them. And they cast out many demons, and anointed with oil many who were sick, and <u>healed</u> them. Mark 6:5, 13 (NKJV)

    And Jesus said to him, "I will come and heal him." Matthew 8:7 (NKJV)

Note: *Therapeuo* can also be translated as, 'household' Revelation 22:2 TPWT

8. *Iama* (NT:2386) means a cure (the effect); healing; repairing. It is translated in the KJV as: healing. (See also Appendix Two)

    To another faith by the same Spirit; to another the <u>gifts of healing</u> by the same Spirit. 1 Corinthians 12:9 (KJV)

Have all the gifts of healing? do all speak with tongues? do all interpret? 1 Corinthians 12:30 (KJV)

9. *Iaomai* (NT:2390) means to cure (literally or figuratively). It is translated in the KJV as: heal; make whole. (See also Appendix Two)

Immediately the fountain of her blood was dried up, and she felt in her body that she was <u>healed</u> of the affliction. Mark 5:29 NKJV

How God anointed Jesus of Nazareth with the Holy Spirit and with power, who went about doing good and <u>healing</u> all who were oppressed by the devil, for God was with Him. Acts 10:38 (NKJV)

10. *Iasis* (NT:2392) means the act of curing. It is translated in the KJV as: cure; heal; healing.

And He said to them, "Go, tell that fox, 'Behold, I cast out demons and perform <u>cures</u> today and tomorrow, and the third day I shall be perfected." Luke 13:32 (NKJV)

11. *Hugiaino* (NT:5198) means to have sound health; be well (in body); to be uncorrupt (true in doctrine). It is translated in the KJV as: be in health; be safe and sound; whole; be whole; wholesome.

Beloved, I pray that you may prosper in all things and be in <u>health,</u> just as your soul prospers. 3 John 2 (NKJV)

11. *Hugies* (NT:5199) means healthy: well; well in body; true (in doctrine). It is translated in the KJV as: sound; whole.

And He said to her, "Daughter, your faith has made you well. Go in peace, and be <u>healed</u> of your affliction." Mark 5:34 NKJV

So the multitude marveled when they saw the mute speaking, the maimed <u>made whole</u>, the lame walking, and the blind seeing; and they glorified the God of Israel. Matthew 5:31 (NKJV)

13 *Sozo* (NT:4982) means: to save; deliver; protect; heal; preserve; make whole. It is translated in the KJV as: heal, preserve, save (self), do well, be (make) whole. Sozo is used 86 times in reference to saving the soul, but in the verse below it refers to saving the physical body and healing it of sickness and disease:

For she said to herself, "If only I may touch His garment, I shall be made well." But Jesus turned around, and when He saw her He said, "Be of good cheer, daughter; your faith has <u>made you well</u>." And the woman was <u>made well</u> from that hour. Matthew 9:21-22 (NKJV)

Wherever He entered, into villages, cities, or the country, they laid the sick in the marketplaces, and begged Him that they might just touch the hem of His garment. And as many as touched Him were <u>made well</u>. Mark 6:56 (NKJV)

14. *Diasozo* (NT:1295) means: to save thoroughly; to heal thoroughly; to cure; preserve; rescue; make perfectly whole; etc. It is translated in the KJV as: bring safe; escape (safe); heal; make perfectly whole; save. It is used of the body being healed.

And besought him that they might only touch the hem of his garment: and as many as touched were <u>made perfectly whole.</u> Matthew 14:36 (KJV)

So when he heard about Jesus, he sent elders of the Jews to Him, pleading with Him to come and <u>heal</u> his servant. And a certain centurion's servant, who was dear to him, was sick and ready to die. Now when He concluded all His sayings in the hearing of the people, He entered Capernaum. Luke 7:1-3 (NKJV)

APPENDIX TWO:
IAOMI & IAMA

Strong's Exhaustive Concordance:

- **G2390** ἰάομαι *Iaomai* **Total KJV Occurrences:** 29

- **G2386** ἴαμα *iama* **Total KJV Occurrences:** 3 (1 Cor. 12:9,28,30) "a healing" (the result of the act)

- The above words have been <u>underlined</u> in the verses below

Iaomai was the healing approach Jesus used almost exclusively. It is instantaneous miracle healing which involves a release of divine healing power, and is often coupled with casting out demons, thus overcoming the forces of darkness and manifesting the Kingdom of God. I would view *Iaomai* (instant miracles) as a sub-category within *therapeuo*.

- **Defined from Kittle (**Theological Dictionary of the New Testament) - *to heal, healing, healer*
- **A Working Definition of *Iaomai*** - *Iaomai is the power of God which releases miraculous healing and casting out of demons.*

As you meditate on the verses below, you may want to use the 7 Step Meditation Process suggested by Communion with God Ministries. [1] I suggest that you read the surrounding verses; then prayerfully journal what God is speaking to you about how to increase the healing power of the Gospel that flows through your hands to those who are sick. After recording these insights, summarize them and practice them in your group or with those you meet in your

184

daily life. Healing can be done anywhere. Jesus did it, and a modern example of a man doing it is Pete Cabrera.[2]

Verses with *Iaomai* or *Iama*:
1. *But the centurion said, "Lord, I am not worthy for You to come under my roof, but just say the word, and my servant will be <u>healed</u>." (Matt. 8:8 NASB)*

2. *And Jesus said to the centurion, "Go; it shall be done for you as you have believed." And the servant was <u>healed</u> that very moment. (Matt. 8:13 NASB)*

3. *For the heart of this people has become dull, with their ears they scarcely hear, and they have closed their eyes, otherwise they would see with their eyes, hear with their ears, and understand with their heart and return, and I would <u>heal</u> them. (Matt. 13:15 NASB)*

4. *Then Jesus said to her, "O woman, your faith is great; it shall be done for you as you wish." And her daughter was <u>healed</u> at once. (Matt. 15:28 NASB)*

5. *Immediately the flow of her blood was dried up; and she felt in her body that she was <u>healed</u> of her affliction. (Mk. 5:29 NASB)*

6. *The Spirit of the Lord is upon me, because he hath anointed me to preach the gospel to the poor; he hath sent me to <u>heal</u> the brokenhearted, to preach deliverance to the captives, and recovering of sight to the blind, to set at liberty them that are bruised, (Lk. 4:18 KJV)*

7. *One day He was teaching; and there were some Pharisees and teachers of the law sitting there, who had come from every village of Galilee and Judea and*

from Jerusalem; and the power of the Lord was present for Him to perform <u>healing</u>. (Lk. 5:17 NASB)

8. *...who had come to hear Him and to be <u>healed</u> of their diseases; and those who were troubled with unclean spirits were being cured (therapeuo). (Lk. 6:17b,18 NASB)*

9. *And all the people were trying to touch Him, for power was coming from Him and <u>healing</u> them all. (Lk. 6:19 NASB)*

10. *For this reason I did not even consider myself worthy to come to You, but just say the word, and my servant will be <u>healed</u>. (Lk. 7:7 NASB)*

11. *When the woman saw that she had not escaped notice, she came trembling and fell down before Him, and declared in the presence of all the people the reason why she had touched Him, and how she had been immediately <u>healed</u>. (Lk. 8:47 NASB)*

12. *And He sent them out to proclaim the kingdom of God and to perform <u>healing</u>. (Lk. 9:2 NASB)*

13. *But the crowds were aware of this and followed Him; and welcoming them, He began speaking to them about the kingdom of God and <u>curing</u> (iaomai) those who had need of healing (therapeia). (Lk. 9:11 NASB)*

14. *While he was still approaching, the demon slammed him to the ground and threw him into a convulsion. But Jesus rebuked the unclean spirit, and <u>healed</u> the boy and gave him back to his father. (Lk. 9:42 NASB)*

15. *Now one of them, when he saw that he had been <u>healed</u>, turned back, glorifying God with a loud voice, (Lk. 17:15 NASB)*

16. *But Jesus answered and said, "Stop! No more of this." And He touched his ear and <u>healed</u> him. (Lk. 22:51 NASB)*

17. *When he heard that Jesus had come out of Judea into Galilee, he went to Him and was imploring Him to come down and <u>heal</u> his son; for he was at the point of death. (Jn. 4:47 NASB)*

18. *But the man who was <u>healed</u> did not know who it was, for Jesus had slipped away while there was a crowd in that place. (Jn. 5:13 NASB)*

19. *"He has blinded their eyes and he hardened their heart, so that they would not see with their eyes and perceive with their heart, and be converted and I <u>heal</u> them." (Jn. 12:40 NASB)*

20. *Peter said to him, "Aeneas, Jesus Christ <u>heals</u> you; get up and make your bed." Immediately he got up. (Acts 9:34 NASB)*

21. *"You know of Jesus of Nazareth, how God anointed Him with the Holy Spirit and with power, and how He went about doing good and <u>healing</u> all who were oppressed by the devil, for God was with Him." (Acts 10:38 NASB)*

22. *And it happened that the father of Publius was lying in bed afflicted with recurrent fever and dysentery; and Paul went in to see him and after he had prayed, he laid his hands on him and <u>healed</u> him. (Acts 28:8 NASB)*

23. *To another faith by the same Spirit, and to another gifts of <u>healing</u> by the one Spirit, (1 Cor. 12:9 NASB)*

24. *And God has appointed in the church, first apostles, second prophets, third teachers, then miracles, then gifts of <u>healings</u>, helps, administrations, various kinds of tongues. (1 Cor. 12:28 NASB)*

25. *All do not have gifts of <u>healings</u>, do they? All do not speak with tongues, do they? All do not interpret, do they? (1 Cor. 12:30 NASB)*

26. *And make straight paths for your feet, so that the limb which is lame may not be put out of joint, but rather be <u>healed.</u> (Heb. 12:13 NASB)*

27. *Therefore, confess your sins to one another, and pray for one another so that you may be <u>healed</u>. The effective prayer of a righteous man can accomplish much. (Jas 5:16 NASB)*

28. *And He Himself bore our sins in His body on the cross, so that we might die to sin and live to righteousness; for by His wounds you were <u>healed</u>. (1 Pet. 2:24 NASB)*

This word refers mostly to physical healing although it can refer to healing the heart also. These healings are essentially instantaneous and coupled with the laying on of hands and casting out of demons. Healing is enhanced by confessing sins one to another, and faith, and touching. There is a power to heal that is transmitted and released through the laying on of hands. Casting out of demons was considered in Luke 6:18 to be a cure (*therapeuo*) rather than a healing (*Iaomai*).

---

[1] https://www.cwgministries.org/blogs/steps-biblical-meditation
[2] https://www.youtube.com/user/kwisatz73